PRAISE for JEANNIE

"I was riveted. Janyne generously [...] her process of healing from her own [...] perspective of her childhood parts wh[...] [...] to cope at the time, as well as from the perspective of the wise adult Janyne who loves these children as they should have been loved then. If you want a real-time glimpse into the minds and hearts of children who are living their truths of coping with maternal neglect, read this book. If you want a deeper understanding of childhood trauma and healing, read this book."

–LIZ HUNTER, Marriage and Family Therapist

"With creativity and honesty, Janyne McConnaughey goes deep. Using a narrative approach to explore pain, trauma, and healing, Janyne carries her readers along with insightful prose. This is a great followup to *Brave*!"

–THOMAS JAY OORD, author of *God Can't: How to Believe in God and Love After Tragedy, Abuse, and Other Evils*

"Janyne has a gift for taking us into her rabbit hole and helping us understand the challenges of healing from trauma. I strongly recommend this book to educators who wish to understand their students who may be dissociating in their class. Thanks to Janyne's transparent telling of her own story, the complex concept of dissociation can be understood without needing a psychology degree."

–MELISSA SADIN, exec. director of Ducks & Lions, program director of ATN Creating Trauma Sensitive Schools, author of *Teachers Guide to Trauma*

"Janyne McConnaughey continues writing her way into our hearts with her new book, *Jeannie's Brave Childhood*, a fantastical weaving of story, instruction and resilience. As a wounded healer, Janyne takes us on a journey of healing from trauma and shattering of the self, to re-attachment and wholeness. This is a playful and imaginative labor of love, as insightful and hope-filled as her previous book in the series, *Brave*."

–LON MARSHALL, Marriage and Family Therapist

"Janyne cleverly interweaves the story of her childhood selves with that of Alice and her trip to Wonderland. This heart-wrenching, harrowing, hopeful story has changed the way I approach ministry. A must read for those who hope to minister effectively to the many in their congregations who have experienced childhood trauma."

–SUSAN ARMSTRONG, DM pastor of care and discipleship, Reynoldsburg Church of the Nazarene

"A masterful journey into a human psyche deeply affected by the dragon of trauma. It will undoubtedly help countless others find reassurance, hope, and wholeness. This is candid and gifted storytelling and fascinating integration of the latest findings in trauma research, attachment theory, self-compassion and forgiveness. Janyne's reflections on God in the aftermath of trauma is paradigm shifting and invaluable. This book is not only for those affected by trauma, but also for therapists desiring to understand their heroic clients more deeply and to walk alongside them more effectively."

—MARK KARRIS, author of
Season of Heartbreak: Healing for the Heart, Brain, and Soul

"Dr. McConnaughey has allowed her child selves to share their memories of trauma. Her masterful storytelling set the scenes so wonderfully that I felt as if I were in the room watching her interact with the children. I was compelled to keep reading even though these are truly heart-breaking stories. I would recommend it to anyone who needs a gentler introduction to the reality and lasting effects of childhood sexual abuse and trauma, insecure attachment, and Dissociative Identity Disorders."

—LESLIE R. MIKESELL, Ph.D

"Janyne McConnaughey opens a window into the thought processes of a child in trauma. I am now more knowledgeable and better equipped to teach my students. Thank you, Janyne, for sharing your story and for allowing 'the children' to share their stories too."

—ROSIE LOLESS, elementary school teacher

"Captivating, thrilling, and empowering...For those who wonder if healing is possible...Told from a fanciful yet truly grounded perspective."

—KIERSTEN ADKINS, M.A., LPC, exec. director, Pathway To Hope

"From cover to cover, this book is a masterpiece. Cohesive and expertly crafted. Janyne McConnaughey has taken a childhood of trauma and managed to redeem it to unfold into a gift of hope for those who have experienced childhood abuse. As a lifelong educator, I believe reading this book will enable anyone who works with children to see the unseen, to better recognize and touch with grace the heart of a silent sufferer."

—SUSAN ELAINE JENKINS, author of *Scandalon:
Running from Shame and Finding God's Scandalous Love*

JEANNIE'S BRAVE CHILDHOOD

BEHAVIOR and HEALING
THROUGH the LENS
of
ATTACHMENT and TRAUMA

With love to all future generations of McConnaughey

Janyne

Janyne McConnaughey, Ph.D.

CLADACH
Publishing

JEANNIE'S BRAVE CHILDHOOD : Behavior and Healing through the Lens of Attachment and Trauma

Copyright © 2019 by Janyne McConnaughey

Published by Cladach Publishing
PO Box 336144 Greeley, CO 80633
http://cladach.com

All rights reserved. Printed in the United States of America. No part of this book may be used or reproduced in any manner whatsoever without written permission except in the case of brief quotations embodied in critical articles or reviews.

Cover Design: Kay McConnaughey
Cover Photo of Chair: © joesive47 / Adobe Stock

ISBN: 9781945099120
Library of Congress Control Number: 2018965841

Printed in the United States of America

This book is dedicated to my father,

Kenneth L. Jenkins

whose love for, and belief in me, made all the difference. He was wise, kind, and gentle; with strength of character and the ability to laugh at most anything. In all my writing, I am reminded and inspired by this note found in one of his Bibles, long after he left us:

> *"Joseph Pulitzer deserved his own prize for this advice: 'Put it before them: briefly so they will hear it, clearly so they appreciate it, picturesquely so they will remember it (and above all) accurately so they will be guided by its light.'"*

In this note my father had revised and adapted Pulitzer's actual words to better fit himself as a preacher and person. He had changed "read" to "hear" and then removed the word "forcibly" as it appeared in Pulitzer's original statement:

> *"[I]t's my duty to see that they get the truth; but that's not enough, I've got to put it before them briefly so that they will read it, clearly so that they will understand it, forcibly so that they will appreciate it, picturesquely so that they will remember it, and, above all, accurately so that they may be wisely guided by its light."*

TABLE OF CONTENTS

INTRODUCTION

Jeannie, the composite of all of my child selves,[1] and Alice, of *Alice in Wonderland* fame, were having a conversation. They became close friends during the writing of this book, but they first met during the writing of *BRAVE: A Personal Story of Healing Childhood Trauma*. The insights the two provided were instrumental to my writing; and on this day, Jeannie expressed a concern for the readers.

"I hope the readers are familiar with the story of Wonderland. They kind of need to be."

"Yes, I agree!" Alice responded. "I hope they know about the White Rabbit, falling down rabbit holes, and finding keys. Oh, and I hope they understand about growing and shrinking!"

"And," Jeannie continued, "the dormouse, the March Hare, the Cheshire Cat, the Duchess, the Queen and her Gardeners, as well as the Mad Hatter's Tea Party. This book will make more sense to them if they know about those!"

Alice and Jeannie had a point. They looked up at me and giggled as Jeannie said, "I bet they wonder why there's an armchair on the cover."

Alice laughed and said, "Because we are all mad here!"

---

1. My dissociative child parts are identified as "child selves" to emphasize they are all "me." They were not created to tell my story. They surfaced during therapy with distinct personalities.

Yes, there were times I felt that way! My inner child developed in multiple split parts and used the fantasies of her childhood to survive. The story of Alice was one such fantasy. Alice was an expert at survival—just like Jeannie.

Alice's story is as interwoven in this book as it was in my childhood, during my years of teaching children's literature, and in my eclectic office décor. The inner world I built in order to survive my childhood trauma was as creative as the pain was deep. The lines between fantasy and reality were often blurred during my childhood, during healing, and now within the pages of this book. For "black vs. white" or "fantasy vs. reality" thinkers this may be problematic, but it is an essential component in understanding hurting children.

My purpose in using storytelling and fanciful settings is to help the reader view the often difficult situations children experience with a childlike perspective. Seeing trauma and survival through the child's eyes helps us to understand their needs-based behaviors. The child has few strategies for survival beyond his or her own imagination.

The story of childhood sexual abuse[2] that is fully explained in *BRAVE* is foundational, but not essential, to this book (see Addendum I: Synopsis of *BRAVE*). My insecure attachment and abuse resulted in a life lived via dissociative coping strategies. Often mistaken as "mad," splitting off parts in order to survive is a completely normal response to childhood abuse.

---

2. It is possible that readers who have experienced sexual abuse as children may be occasionally triggered by some content in this book. Please seek professional care. This book is not intended to act as a self-help guide to healing, but it may provide helpful insights for individuals in therapy.

My story unfolded during several years of intensive therapy. I didn't process my childhood memories as an adult remembering what happened. My dissociated child selves sat on the therapy couch inside my adult body and processed with Dr. Sue (Dr. Susan Kwiecien—see her Foreword to *BRAVE* in Addendum II of this book).

For the sake of my readers, I have done my very best to make it clear when I, one of my child selves, or Alice is talking. Should anyone be confused, that confusion will serve to illustrate the complicated inner world of traumatized children. I couldn't always be absolutely sure who was talking. In the following pages my child selves sometimes blend, go by different names, and pop up unexpectedly. Really, Alice is the only one who seemed to fully understand all the child selves were actually one child named Jeannie.

Occasionally, one of the three adult selves (that I called "the Three Chairs") who lived my life as a college professor/teacher educator steps in to speak. Non Janyne originally wrote this Introduction in a style that sounded decidedly like a college lecture. She agreed to this revision but insisted that every book should have objectives. Knowing full well this is like the first night of class when I would read the syllabus—though students (and readers!) just want to get on with it—I will humor Non Janyne and state here that my objectives are:

1) to use my personal story as a window to the internalized messages and developmental effects of disrupted attachment and trauma.

2) to view misunderstood behaviors through the lens of trauma and attachment.

3) to explain and illustrate the role of healing as essential in fostering self-compassion; as a path to creating

behavioral change; and as a precursor to forgiveness.

4) to illustrate avenues of healing through therapy (including EMDR[3]), conversations (self talk), storytelling (live and written), literature, play, and reframing.

There we have it. And now, my readers—and Alice—are waiting.

'I don't see how [s]he can ever finish, if [s]he doesn't begin.' But she waited patiently.
 —Alice[4]

3. Both professional and client-oriented information about EMDR (Eye Movement Desensitization and Reprocessing) is available at EMDR Institute, Inc. http://www.emdr.com/

4. All quotes attributed to Alice are taken from *Alice's Adventures in Wonderland,* written by English mathematician Charles Lutwidge Dodgson under the pseudonym Lewis Carroll, and first published in 1865.

PART I
MY CHILD SELVES GO TO THERAPY

I almost wish I hadn't gone down that rabbit
hole—and yet—and yet—it's rather curious, you
know this sort of life! I do wonder what can have
happened to me. When I used to read fairy tales,
I fancied that kind of thing never happened, and
now here I am in the middle of one!

–Alice

During the year in which I processed the trauma held inside my child selves, Jeannie, as the Storyteller, begged to tell *BRAVE* in her own way. Her story is told here. Part I gives Jeannie's creative version of *BRAVE*. The gathering described provides an overview of my dissociative system and how my dissociated "selves" learned to process together. Part I concludes with a series of memories not included in *BRAVE*. These memories were essential to knowing my true self—a crucial part of healing and understanding many of my attachment and trauma-related behaviors.

I have chosen not to fully share the details of the sexual abuse included in the following chapters. The cognitive transcriptions of the memories as experienced during therapy with the use of EMDR (you'll find these memories indented and italicized throughout this book) somewhat portray the depth of the trauma. The processing was sensory, physical, and emotional. Imaginative storytelling helped my child selves process the pain of the memories.

Alice (of *Alice in Wonderland*) quickly became part of this processing. I truly admired her ability to fall down a rabbit hole and still keep her wits about her.

Since my childhood revolved around the church, naturally God would be part of Jeannie's storytelling. Jeannie and God talked quite often as I wrote, and God sometimes spoke in a voice which was decidedly "therapist-esque."

Despite most of my abuse occurring within the context of people connected with the church, my child selves never seemed to question God's love for them—protection yes, but not love. This is not true for so many abused children. My childlike faith was in part due to my father, whose preaching painted a picture of a loving God.

Thus, we begin with Jeannie and God having a conversation. The adult "me" occasionally wanders through to fill in gaps and is sometimes reminded that this is not *my* story to tell.

1
JEANNIE AND GOD MAKE A PLAN

There was a hush in Heaven as God looked at a small child inside a grown-up body. The angels knew, when this child spoke, it was going to be interesting. They seldom heard others talk to God exactly like she did. No matter her age, no matter what happened to her, she was always determined to live. Most importantly, she believed God loved her.

She was getting impatient with her pain. This was going to be a significant conversation. She seemed to be yelling at her adult self, who was obviously ignoring her.

Jeannie and God Have a Talk

First, Jeannie tried talking to adult Janyne. "Hello, up there!"

(I, adult Janyne, heard nothing.)

"Do you not see me down here inside you?"

(I heard nothing.)

"Do you know why you can't stand in lines? Do you know why you have panic attacks? Do you know why you wake up with a feeling of dread every morning? Do you know why you collapse and need to go to bed?"

(I heard nothing, because the buzz in my head was much too loud; the conversations were too many.)

"I have the answers you have looked for all your life. Let me lead you to them. Hello! *Hello! Helloooooooo!*"

(I still heard nothing.)

The small child inside the adult who wasn't listening, sighed with exasperation.

"God, she isn't listening to me. She doesn't even know she is shifting and living in parts. She doesn't know what the dark cloud is and why she gets so depressed."

God looked at her with compassion. "Jeannie, she doesn't know. She only knows what she allows herself to know, and you aren't part of that."

Jeannie, standing tall and proud, answered, "Jesus told the disciples not to ignore children, but she is ignoring me."

God smiled at her spunkiness. "You make a good point, Jeannie. Adults often ignore the child inside of them. It is time to help her. How do you think we can get her attention?"

"Well, you are God, you know," she answered indignantly.

God laughed and watched as Jeannie thought about the question.

"Remember when she was in the long hallway and read a verse about children?" asked Jeannie. "She felt you then. She knew you were trying to tell her to take care of the children, but she didn't understand we were inside of her. It was like your presence was surrounding her. You could try that again."

"Very good plan ... and in a car. She does seem to sense me in cars. I know someone who can help her. She is a therapist, and she will listen to your story. Her name is Dr. Susan Kwiecien. You can trust her. She will care about you more than anyone ever has. Some of your child selves have problems trusting, but her care will convince them. It is time; are you ready?"

Jeannie's hands were on her hips and she looked determined. "I've been ready for sixty-one years!"

"Yes, you have." God seemed delighted by her determination.

THE PLAN FOR FALLING DOWN THE RABBIT HOLE

"God, is today the day?" Jeannie asked.

"Do you think she will listen today?"

Jeannie's face looked concerned. "She has been sad because her friend moved. I was sad, too, and she almost heard me crying. The dark cloud swallowed her whole."

"We need to help her, don't we? You are going to be strong and brave. Remember how Alice fell down the rabbit hole in Wonderland?"

"You know I do!" There was a decided look of anticipation on her small face. "It sounded like so much fun to go down a rabbit hole. Is that where we are going?"

God smiled at her eagerness and was glad she didn't fully understand what was ahead of her. "Well it isn't exactly a rabbit hole, but it is going to feel like one to her. You aren't afraid; but she will be. You know the part of you who wants to do what I suggest?"

"Oh yes, *she's* the one who steps in to take gigantic leaps of faith! She wants to do what you feel is best for her!" She was pointing to another one of my child selves standing in a nearby shadow.

The child stepped out of the shadow and looked inquisitive as God began to explain the plan to her.

"Well, it is always your choice, you know, but you will need to step in and make the phone call when I prompt her to call her friend's therapist. It will be important to make the phone call; but she will have difficulty doing so and will be afraid; so she will need you."

Jeannie, the Storyteller, looked at her twin sister called the Warrior, who was given the task. They seemed to communicate without speaking. They knew the Warrior could do this, but they were still a bit confused.

Then, together as the child called Nine,[1] they inquired, "So, you are going to simply let her feel your presence and she will know who to call? Can you do that?"

God laughed. "I am God, you know. And she really does listen to me." He looked at the warrior part of Nine and said, "You will help her be strong and make the phone call."

She seemed to stand taller in the importance of her job.

And with this, the plan was ready.

Adult Janyne listened, and the Warrior gave her courage.

This was how we all **fell down a rabbit hole** in Dr. Sue's office.

> *In another moment Alice went down ... never once considering how in the world she was to get out again.*
> —Alice

---

1. Nine, the Warrior, didn't reveal her twin, the Storyteller, until much later. During most of therapy this part of me was known as Nine and only showed her warrior side. "Nine" indicates the Warrior unless otherwise noted.

2
JUMPING DOWN A RABBIT HOLE

I n the story of *Alice in Wonderland*, as Alice fell down the rabbit hole, she saw cupboards, bookshelves, maps and pictures. She managed to pick up a jar of orange marmalade only to discover it was empty, then set it down in another place. In my story, my first phone conversation with Dr. Sue was similar. I grabbed *many* completely random things to tell her while falling.

Down, down, down the rabbit hole I went … and there was no stopping the fall.

At this point, it is a bit embarrassing to realize how much I needed my strong child selves to help me be brave; but in my defense, there was another side to the story. It really did feel like I fell down a rabbit hole. But there was so much more to it.

LEAPING WITH THE WHITE RABBIT

Looking at the small child who was typing, I asked, "Jeannie, do you mind if I tell my version of the rabbit hole story?"

"Oh, please do. You didn't have any idea what was going on." She giggled, then leaned back to let me type for a while.

With Jeannie looking over my shoulder, I began typing....

೧೨

Standing at the edge of the rabbit hole contemplating my next move, I was sure it was the White Rabbit I was chasing for some time. His urgency felt as if it were my own.

19

The White Rabbit came running past me and checked his watch before he dove into the hole. The ticking of the watch pounded in my ears, but time stood still. Perched between a past life (which felt as if I no longer belonged) and some unknown future, jumping down a rabbit hole seemed like a truly bad idea. One thing for certain, if a splendidly dressed, pink-eyed White Rabbit was part of my future, it was going to be interesting.

Phone number in hand, I took three steps back, and briefly paused to consider what brought me to the edge of the rabbit hole. The day the White Rabbit first crossed my path, the dark cloud overtook me. My life was lovely, but I couldn't enjoy it. The darkness was bumping up against my perfect shell and I was beginning to crack.

Jumping into a rabbit hole was a watershed decision, and it was going to be the bravest of all brave moments of my life. Looking both directions to be sure no one was watching, I braced myself, and began running.... *Leap, Janyne! Make the call! Leap into the depths of the darkness in your soul! Watch your life go by like a movie while you fall deeper and deeper into the rabbit hole. You are in free fall!*

> *Down, down, down. Would the fall never come to an end? 'I wonder how many miles I've fallen by this time!' she said aloud. 'I must be getting somewhere near the centre of the earth.'*
> –Alice

Despite my anxiety, I managed to sound somewhat intelligent during the phone conversation. But I felt as if a floodgate had opened and I was beginning to puke the depths of my soul.

In the middle of my rambling talk on the phone with the

therapist, I blurted, "My mother lived to be 94 and she wore me out." On the other end of the line, I heard only a quiet pause and a listening ear.

When the call ended, I sat down and considered my ramblings. My mother issues were obvious.

JEANNIE WAS LISTENING

"God, did you hear all that? It was like she never talked to anyone before. She told about me, or at least she thought she did; she told about the sad adult stuff. Then she talked about Mother."

"Did you not want her to talk about your mother, Jeannie?" God knew the story.

"She wasn't my mother. I mean, not really. She didn't act like my mother."

God looked concerned. "So you will eventually need to talk about it, won't you?"

"Well, maybe. Will it stop me from looking for a mother? In *Are You My Mother?*[1] the baby bird in the story finds his mother. I never did, you know. That book makes me sad."

"You must be brave. Tell your story as you can. Tell it from the beginning. If you don't remember it exactly, that's OK; tell it as you remember. I will hold you. And Dr. Sue will take care of you."

> *She felt that she was dozing off … when suddenly*
> thump! thump! *Down she came upon a bed of sticks and dry leaves, and the fall was over.*
> –Alice

---

1. Eastman, P.D., *Are You My Mother?* (New York, NY: Random House Children's Books, 1998).

Trying to Open Locked Doors

After several sessions of endless ramblings, it was time to begin incorporating EMDR as part of my therapy. After processing a childhood memory of an interaction with my mother, Dr. Sue asked me to return to my adult self. I heard my own voice ask, "Which one?"

Thump. Thump. Thump. It was a hard landing at the bottom of the rabbit hole, but the fall was somewhat softened by the calm voice of Dr. Sue. Evidently, having people dropping down rabbit holes into her office was a common experience.

I knew immediately that I was living my life as more than one adult self. I recognized my three adult selves, could describe them, and wanted to rid myself of the one who held feelings. It would be months before the three adult selves were able to cooperate and begin helping my child selves.

Many questions I didn't yet know to ask. But I was searching desperately for a doorway to "normal." This three-point landing spot certainly did not resemble "normal" in any way. I wanted out of the pain and confusion, but I needed to find a way to unlock the door to living as a healthy and whole, integrated person.

> *There were doors all round the hall, but they were all locked; and when Alice had been all the way down one side and up the other, trying every door, she walked sadly down the middle, wondering how she was ever to get out again.*
>
> –Alice

I felt like Alice trying all the locked doors and wondering how she would ever get out again, since the key she needed was on the table, and she was too small to reach it. The truth was, the only door that could be unlocked was way too small for my adult self to go through. I would need to become the child within me to open the door to the garden that, in my case, represented healing.

It was some time before I was willing to accept that we were working with child selves and not merely childhood memories. It was even longer before I fully knew the trauma that split me into dissociative parts. But even so, I was finally ready to listen to my inner child.

LISTENING TO JEANNIE AT LAST

"Hello!" yelled the child self within me.

"Hello, Jeannie. I see you now. I am listening," I said.

Now that she had my attention, she began talking so fast, she stumbled over the words. "Well, it is about time! It will be so much easier to tell my story now that we're talking! I've been trying to get your attention. And I am not the only one, you know. You met some of us, but you thought we were memories."

Whoa! I was listening more intently now. She seemed to have a lot she wanted to tell me. Yet, I still felt the need to explain why I hadn't been listening.

"It was difficult adjusting to three adult parts of 'me.' Then, pulling them together was a lot of work and took some time. Now that the adults have integrated, we can help *you*. Do you want to tell your story from the beginning?"

Jeannie looked at me with a serious expression and began slowly. "Yes, I can tell the story; but sometimes you'll have to become me to understand. Only one of us can be the one who is living." She looked at me as if it might be too much for me to understand. Possibly she was right. It was a bit unsettling to think I would sometimes need to be a child. How was that going to work?

"I kind of understand I will sometimes need to be a child to process the memory, but at other times I'll need to be an adult," I told her.

"OK, then. When you need to be big, you can eat the cake."

"The cake?"

"Yes, when you need to be big, just eat the cake. You know, like in *Alice in Wonderland*." She picked up the book sitting next to her and began reading about the cake.

> *Soon her eye fell on a little glass box that was lying under the table. She opened it, and found in it a very small cake, on which the words 'EAT ME' were beautifully marked in currants.*
> –Alice

It was going to be essential to suspend my adult logic and reasoning if I wanted to help the child selves inside of me. And so, we came to an agreement. When I needed to be an adult, I would "eat the cake." The cake was the symbol for "I see you. Stay right here; I will be back, but for now I need to be an adult." This technique worked most of the time. Life got extremely complicated, though, and from moment to moment, it was never clear who I actually was.

> *I wonder if I've changed in the night? Let me think: was I the same when I got up this morning? I almost think I can remember feeling a little different. But if I'm not the same, the question is 'Who in the world am I?'*
> –Alice

Truly—who was I? That became less and less certain. By the time we found all the child selves who were frozen by the trauma, it was evident I knew very little when I plummeted down the rabbit hole.

Jeannie Steps In Again

"Wait!" It was Jeannie again. "You are not telling this story. I am!" She laughed at me, knowing how hard it was for me to leave things in the capable hands of my child selves. But she seemed eager to tell me something.

"What is it, Jeannie?"

"Well, you remember the first year with the Three Chairs?"

Oh, yes. The memory of the first year of therapy was still vivid! When anyone mentioned the Three Chairs, it always referred to my three adult selves: Janyne, Non Janyne, and Jane.

She continued. "You never knew who was telling the memories. You thought *you* were remembering, but you weren't. We children were the ones who held the memories. You couldn't have helped the Three Chairs without us! It was *our* memories you needed to process."

This made sense. One day I had sat on my hands and refused to do therapy. And quite often the most surprisingly childlike things came out of my mouth. She was right. I had been shifting to small child selves for some time without realizing it.

Jeannie laughed. "You never really knew who you were."

This was certainly true. Often during therapy I shifted for significant portions of the session, but I didn't realize this until sometime later. So confusing!

> 'Who are you?' said the Caterpillar.
> 'I ... I hardly know, Sir, just at present—at least I
> know who I was when I got up this morning, but I think
> I must have been changed several times since then.'
> —Alice

It would be two years before my entire dissociative system of child selves arrived in my conscious awareness for healing—two complicated, overwhelming years. But in the end, I finally knew who I was.

3
GATHERING IN THE KITCHEN

'But I don't want to go among mad people,' Alice remarked.
'Oh, you can't help that,' said the Cat, 'we're all mad here.'
—Alice

B*RAVE*, my first book and the companion volume to this one, explains the trauma that caused my dissociative splits. This present book brings into focus the behaviors that resulted from that trauma and from unmet needs. The gathering in this chapter introduces the parts of my dissociative system—a family picture of sorts.

During this gathering, a child self identified as Five, arrived. She had hidden much longer than we had believed possible (until after I finalized the content for *BRAVE*). Five's story was pivotal in understanding many of my childhood behaviors.

The setting in which I learned Five's story, one of the three settings in which my process gatherings took place, was a kitchen. The cast arrived in the general order in which each child self surfaced during therapy.

Meeting in the Kitchen

The adults, known as the Three Chairs, came to the kitchen to reflect on our journey and prepare a dinner for those who would soon arrive. Non Janyne was straightening the kitchen, while Janyne worked on decorating name cards and placemats. Jane, as always, was holding the small infant.

My husband, Scott, was cooking. He was glad to see the Three Chairs working together so well. A lot of healing had taken place to bring these three into a spirit of cooperation. Now Non Janyne could be in charge without being controlling. Janyne could laugh and enjoy life while accepting the pain she experienced. Jane could care for the infant without fearing that her emotions and feelings would implode our life.

All three looked up to see the two six-year-old twins enter the kitchen. The One Who Cried in the Bed held a box of Kleenex™, which she set on the counter, in case she needed to cry. Her sister, the One Who Lived, saw cookies ready for decorating and started planning designs as she motioned for her twin to join her. Everyone was glad the one twin no longer needed to stay in the bed and cry.

There was a commotion as two ten-year-old twins walked in the door holding the hands of three smaller child selves, who appeared to be about two, three, and four. The Older Sibling helped them off with their coats and hung them up while her sister, the Comforter, applied a Band-Aid™ to the owie of one, gave a white puppy to the next, and wrapped a blanket around the third.

One child self, who appeared to be three, sat on the floor to play with the blocks provided by the Older Sibling. Everyone smiled to see that she was playing again. Then I saw a shadow watching over her. The small child looked up, talked to the shadow, and then returned to playing. The healed Watcher, who began life as the four-year-old's imaginary friend, was still quite protective (but not controlling) of this younger sibling.

It wasn't long until the six-year-old One Who Lives finished decorating her cookies and started helping the small child stack—and then knock over—the blocks. Their laughter filled the room.

A discussion could be heard in the next room. A look of understanding passed among the Three Chairs. The Problem Solver and her sister had arrived. They were continually working on problems and, now that one of them didn't need to run and deposit shame in the basement, they were putting their thinking skills to better uses. They spotted the jigsaw puzzle in the corner, waved to the others, and set to work.

I heard the music before seeing the next two child selves. They timidly peeked in the door. Jane handed the infant to Non Janyne and walked over to lead them in. The seven-year-old twins had arrived. One held a hammer and the other a box, which they carried wherever they went, even though they no longer needed to box up and seal memories in the Cave of Memories. Now they used them to build shelves for new memory boxes and the memories we now knew how to process.

Music followed the two Sevens wherever they went; it filled the room with joy as they asked Janyne if they could help decorate the table. They both had an artistic eye and loved to create settings for memories.

There was a crashing sound. Everyone looked up to see a nine-year-old ride her bike into the room. She looked back at everyone as if defying them to tell her the bike needed to stay outside. No one did. Nine (the one who became the Warrior) and her bike, Bluebird, just went together. They were glad she was now free to ride!

Non Janyne asked, "Where is your sister?"

Nine grinned impishly. "What sister?"

They all laughed. She had hidden her sister, the Storyteller, to the very last. They knew the Storyteller was probably off writing a story or reading a book. She'd be along eventually.

Car headlights shone through the window. The teen and young adult selves known as the Jane-and-Janyne twins had arrived. Ten, the Comforter, looked concerned when she heard the car skid on the gravel; but Jane put her hand on Ten's shoulder and reminded her they were fine and she didn't need to drive for them anymore. The child looked relieved and ran out to talk to the Jane-and-Janyne twins making their way to the kitchen.

Everyone gathered around the table, but one seat was empty. It seemed the Storyteller still hadn't arrived. Then I looked in front of me and saw her hands on my keyboard. She had been in the room the whole time! Sometimes, when she was writing, she simply felt like me.

We could now sit down to celebrate.

Watching the group at the table, I considered how different this gathering would have looked three years earlier. How enjoyable now to watch them interact as healed parts!

LOOKING TO THE PAST

Before therapy, gatherings of this group looked completely different. Non Janyne was very much in control and angry with Janyne for being so frivolous. Jane was in the other room crying because the other two Chairs didn't want her there. She was always holding the infant, and they both felt the rejection to the depth of their being.

The smallest child selves were almost hidden under the dark cloud, and the exhausted Watcher stood outside at the gate trying to protect them. He was slowly collapsing under the strain. The child selves never received an invitation into the kitchen.

In a back bedroom one six-year-old child self was crying while her sister went outside to play and refused to stay in the house for fear of her mother, who had died over five years earlier.

One of the Sevens was hammering more nails in the boards to keep the painful memories contained in the Cave of Memories, while her sister tried to keep the lids on the boxes filled with pain. Their anxiety was overwhelming.

The Eights, who believed the dark cloud was sin, couldn't escape from the dark Basement of Shame.

Nine, an angry warrior with memories of trauma embedded in her body, spent her days guarding her sister who had lost her voice.

The exhausted Tens were doing their best to care for the younger child selves and were desperate to find someone to care about them.

The teens and young adults were sitting at the table drowning in shame but still telling happy stories of our life—without any joy.

Scott as always, was cooking—but was confused by the constantly shifting faces of the wife he called Janyne.

Yes, it was a difficult three years that changed my life forever, as evidenced in the many contrasts between the past and present gatherings.

An Unexpected Visitor

The front door opened and closed. Everyone turned at the sound of small footsteps coming into the kitchen. In front of us stood a child self I had never seen—or at least not recognized. She appeared to be about five years old. Holding out my arms, I pulled her into my lap and leaned close to hear what she was whispering.

"I didn't want to come and heal because I thought Dr. Sue would leave us if we were healed. She wanted you to be my 'mother' but I didn't ever trust mothers."

When she looked up to see Dr. Sue standing in the doorway, she began to cry, "Please don't leave me."

Dr. Sue came in, took the child's hands, and looked into her eyes.

This child needed to know that I, not Dr. Sue, would always be there for her; but she was not yet ready to trust me.

Five began to tell her story about going to a birthday party and how her parents were late picking her up. She told how the birthday girl and her mother had needed to leave. She had begged them not to leave her there with the father she didn't trust.

Then she stopped abruptly and mumbled, "I don't remember any more."

She knew some of the story, and was willing to tell it, but would need help in processing the remainder of the still-buried memory.

As she talked, I was still adjusting to having been completely unaware she existed. She was the part of me who struggled to be independent. I kept pulling tissues from the box brought by the One Who Cries. I pulled out one for the child I now recognized as Five, then one for me, then another for her and another for me. I understood why this child self could not trust me to be the mother she had always needed, since I had removed myself from her pain for so many years. In a sense, I had left her just like our mother had. Again a mother who should have protected her walked out a door. No wonder she feared being left.

Everyone was startled when Non Janyne began to cry. "This was who I was trying to control?" she exclaimed. "I am so sorry, Five. No wonder you didn't want Dr. Sue to leave you. I promise not to leave you!"[1]

Five studied her for a few minutes. Non Janyne often

---

1. The intensity of childhood emotions, especially when created by trauma, is far beyond our capacity to comprehend, and the child is not developmentally capable of "making sense of it" (if such a thing is possible). My black cloud was this explosive emotional turmoil that I simultaneously ran from and tried to control.

reminded her of her own mother, but it seemed she was not the same person now, or she wouldn't be crying. She had never seen her own mother cry.

Looking around the table, Five said, "No, I don't think any of you would have left me."

Everyone murmured in agreement.

It was complicated. Children often cry when left. As a preschool director myself, I saw children cry quite often when parents left. It was normal. Yet, I do wonder if anyone ever saw the deep distress and fear in me. This child self who cried not to be left was going to need some attention. For now, we needed to make a place for her at the table—and a place for Dr. Sue right next to her. We were still going to need our therapist's help.

The Older Sibling, smiling at me across the table, said, "You thought you had found all your child selves. But you hadn't." She was clearly amused.

Five grinned. "I was the best hider," she said.

"Yes," I responded. "And you almost got left out of this book! That would have been a tragic omission!"

Non Janyne Organizes the Seating Arrangement

Non Janyne was squirming. With the addition of two more guests, Adult Janyne's haphazard seating arrangement seemed less than functional. I thought I might as well address the problem.

"Non Janyne, you seem a bit restless. Do you need something?"

What she usually needed was organization. I was right, and as she explained the problem, she was much more diplomatic than her previous self would have been.

"Well, Janyne set a wonderful table. The decorations and place cards are lovely! I am just not sure, with the arrival of our additional guests, whether we are sitting in the best places to help those who might need help." She made a good point.

We agreed, so she took out a sheet of paper and began to draw up a seating arrangement. First she made a list of all the parts of "me" by age.

- *Infant*
- *Two*
- *Three*
- *Four*
- *Five*
- *Six (both the One Who Lives & the One Who Cries)*
- *Seven (Girl with the Hammer & Keeper of the Cave of Memories)*
- *Eight (Problem Solver & Girl in the Basement of Shame—now moved to the Attic of Hope)*
- *Nine (Warrior & Storyteller)*
- *Ten (Older Sibling & Comforter)*
- *Teens Janyne & Jane*
- *Young Adults Janyne & Jane*
- *The Three Chairs (Non Janyne, Jane, & Janyne)*

Then she wrote down *Janyne* (indicating me) and *Dr. Sue*. (And The Watcher was a shadow figure who didn't need to eat.)

"There!' Non Janyne proclaimed. "We need 24 places at the table."

"Does Scott get to sit down?" I laughingly asked.

"Oh! Of course! Then there are 25. I really like the number 25. It is a square number!"

Everyone laughed because Non Janyne had taught math for so many years, it was just a part of who she was. We could see the wheels turning in her head. The big table was made up of smaller tables so it could be arranged various ways.

"We have eight square tables. I'm not sure we need so many." She pulled out her teaching bag and got out the color tiles.[2] The Problem Solver, a much younger version of Non Janyne, headed toward the pile of tiles immediately. Three asked if she could have the cubes instead and sat down on the floor to build a tower.

The problem reminded Non Janyne of the logic puzzles she and my dad loved. My dissociative system was built on developmental stages, but many common traits tied them together over my lifespan. My love for puzzles was one of those. This did seem like a logic puzzle.

Eight, the Problem Solver, becoming interested in the idea of a puzzle, began to help Non Janyne. Finally they announced the solution and began to move the name cards around the table. As everyone settled into their places, we noticed a large, empty armchair at one end of the table, between me and Five.

The Storyteller giggled. "It's there for Alice. Don't you see her?"

> *The table was a large one, but the three were all crowded together at one corner of it: 'No room! No room!' they cried out when they saw Alice coming. 'There's PLENTY of room!' said Alice indignantly, and she sat down in a large armchair at one end of the table.*
>
> –Alice

---

2. This nod to mathematics is for all my former adult math students who were surprised to realize they enjoyed learning math via the use of manipulatives.

4
TABLE CONVERSATIONS

By the time everyone gathered around the table, they understood the structure of my dissociative system and the full story of how they survived and healed. With the surfacing of Five, it seemed we found the child self who lived before the dissociative splits began to create twins within my subconscious. Though I didn't know her full story yet, I sensed Five held the reason why I began splitting into dissociated child selves. She needed to find a way to make the trauma "not happen" so she could get up the next day as if it hadn't.

In her mind, it really didn't matter what had happened to her; behaving was what was important. The prime directives were: 1) appropriate conduct and 2) never talking about what transpired—as if it had never happened. And so it hadn't. This was the cardinal societal and family rule I broke by publishing *BRAVE*.

We had lively discussions around the table. Everyone seemed to be enjoying the evening, even though it didn't go exactly as planned. Over the top of Alice's head, I watched Five. Alice and Five were discussing falling down rabbit holes. They both agreed it was an unsettling experience. Five, whose eyes still held pain, kept glancing at Dr. Sue.

IN THE MIDDLE OF THE LAUGHTER

Laughter erupted at the other end of the table. All eyes turned toward Nine, the Warrior. She was retelling the story of the Sunday she stomped her feet and refused to shake the hand of the hapless church greeter.

"It's funny now," she mused. "But it reminded me of when the neighborhood boys wouldn't let me out of the bedroom."

There was a sudden hush and all eyes were on her. I wondered if she really was OK, but Nine stayed grounded on her chair and didn't float up to the ceiling as she was so apt to do.

Jane[1] asked the question she had learned in therapy: "What are you feeling, Nine?" Jane was the one who often reminded us to consider feelings.

Nine seemed to shiver, and then looked directly at Jane and began talking. "I can remember that day now without floating off somewhere. It was a sad, sad day, but my job was to step in for Ten when she was abused. If I hadn't done this we would have kept splitting every time we were abused."

Jane asked again, "But what are you feeling?"

Nine smiled because she, like all the others, had developed the fine art of talking around any question about feelings. "So I can't get around talking about feelings?" She giggled.

Everyone else laughed rather uncomfortably, glad *they* hadn't been asked the question.

Knowing laughter was often a coping mechanism for avoiding pain, Jane waited.

Nine, sensing Jane's eyes encouraging her to talk, sighed in resignation. She wasn't going to dodge this. "OK, feelings. But first I need to talk to Five." Nine looked over at Five. "I learned how to be brave from *you*. These awful things were just part of our life. No one protected us."

Five and Nine seemed to be the only ones in the room, their connection was so intense. Their character was revealed in the

---

1. The "Janes" and "Janynes" get confusing. From this point on, unless otherwise indicated, "Jane" and "Janyne" are each one of the adult selves (two of the Three Chairs).

set of their chins. They leaned toward each other as Nine continued.

"You didn't have a choice. You were little. You were taught to obey adults. After the party that day, you fought hard not to be left with the bad father; but once the door closed, you were on your own and you knew it. You tried to refuse to drink the beer. You were brave and strong. Afterwards, your being told to drink the beer was all you ever let yourself remember."

This was more than Five had shared earlier. My adult memory of the party in question was odd and emotionless—a party with lots of small children and refusing to drink a smelly drink. *That was it*, I mused, lost in thought.

Five's voice jolted me back to the present. "Yes. I didn't want to be left. He made me drink a lot. Mother made me eat and drink things I didn't want to, so I learned to not taste it and just make it go down my throat."

Nine looked at her with the deepest sadness. "Then you felt funny. Bad things happened. But later you didn't really know if it had happened or not. It was all fuzzy."

Now this vague memory made sense—I had been intoxicated.

Nine moved next to Five and held her hands. This was a side of Nine we hadn't seen before. "It was not your fault," she reassured. "You should have been able to trust adults. They should have protected you. You were strong inside. You had to get up the next day and act like nothing happened. And you didn't apologize."

Everyone older than Five looked around the table at each other. These two knew much more than Five had told us. She had not mentioned an apology.

Leaning toward Dr. Sue, I whispered, "There is more, isn't

there? During therapy, Five must have stopped the memory before it was finished. She didn't tell us everything."

SOMEONE IS CRYING

The distinct sound of stifled tears was coming from somewhere around the table. The One Who Cried no longer held the box of tissues. The box now sat in front of Young Adult Jane whose head was buried in her arms. Her shoulders shook with wrenching sobs she could not contain.

The happy gathering was not turning out as planned; but as I learned in therapy, this processing was "necessary and needed." We would just work through it. Janyne, the young adult who lived, was trying to comfort her twin, but comforting was never her forte. They needed my help.

"Jane, what is it? You are sad. What is bothering you about the conversation between Nine and Five? Can you tell me?"

Young Adult Jane looked at me but still cried.

One of the Sevens stepped forward holding a box. "I can tell you what it is."

Everyone knew the box held another memory. The two seven-year-old twins looked quite serious and somewhat angry. We were unravelling a chain. Well, more like a web. Trauma never only impacts the exact age at which it happens. Instead, it weaves itself in and out of the remainder of a lifetime. Trauma had connected the Sevens and Young Adult Jane.

The young woman in front of me sobbed again but said, "It was the class ... the verse."

This couldn't have been any more confusing. "Please, Sevens, tell me. I don't understand."

The twins began to talk. Sometimes one, then the other, and occasionally both at the same time. "Bad things happened to her. She only wanted someone to help her, but they hurt her instead."

Seven, the one in charge of memories, obviously knew the story, but her sister kept nudging her. "What?" she whispered to her sister. "No, we aren't going to tell *all* of what happened, but this doesn't make sense unless we tell *some* of it."

Seven, the Girl with the Hammer, shrugged but seemed satisfied as her sister continued.

"She took a class in college. It was a Bible class, and they had to read the Song of Solomon. One day she read a verse, and the most awful feeling came over her."

The seven-year-old Girl with the Hammer began to swing it wildly, then pointing to Young Adult Jane, she cried, "That is when you told us to start boarding up the cave!"

Young Adult Jane, her head still on the table, moaned. "I was a swinging door."

Now Nine was sobbing. "I was a swinging door, too!"

It was all so confusing!

"Can someone show me the verse?" I ran to retrieve a Bible from the living room. Before I could pick it up, the small eight-year-old Problem Solver grabbed the Bible and was back at the table flipping the pages to the Song of Solomon. She knew exactly what she was looking for.

"Here it is! The Song of Solomon 8:8-9. In some Bibles, it says a 'swinging door':"

> *We have a little sister, and she has no breasts;*
> *What shall we do for our sister. On the day when she*
> *is spoken for? If she is a wall, we will build on her a*
> *battlement of silver; But if she is a door, we will barricade*
> *her with planks of cedar* (NASB).

The child reading the verse looked both proud and sad as the Sevens stepped up to explain more. "She looked up commentaries. Maybe the boards were to protect the girl. She had no breasts, so she was young like us. But what Young Adult

Jane read in *The Cambridge Bible for Schools and Colleges* only made it worse...."

> *[If she be a wall], i.e. if she resist attacks and preserve her innocence, they will reward her by building upon her a battlement or turret of silver, i.e. they will adorn her, perhaps for her marriage, as the bride in ancient times wore a crown.*
>
> *[And if she be a door], i.e. if she be ready to permit an enemy to pass her defences, then they will fasten her up with a plank of cedar. The meaning is, that as men prevent a door from opening by fastening a plank across so that it cannot move, so they will take measures to prevent her from yielding to her weakness.*

Young Adult Jane moved her chair back, put her head in her lap, and wailed. "I thought I was a swinging door, that I yielded to my weakness or didn't resist the attack. I told Seven to start boarding up the cave entrance to protect men from me!"

I was stunned. Surely this wasn't the meaning. I went back to the living room for my copy of *The Amplified Bible*, which my dad had left me. I hoped it would say the young girl was the one needing protection.

Eight stepped in to read it silently. Then she commented, "You aren't going to like this one, either:"

> *We have a little sister and she has no breasts. What shall we do for our sister on the day when she is spoken for in marriage? If she is a wall [discreet and womanly], we will build upon her a turret [a dowry] of silver; but if she is a door [bold and flirtatious], we will enclose her with boards of cedar.*

Now it was my turn to cry.

Dr. Sue held my hands as I sobbed, "She had no breasts! She was a little girl. They raped her and then called her bold and flirtatious and boarded her up!" My brain was processing at lightning speed now. This tragic memory tied everyone together.

Child self Three crawled into my lap, possibly frightened by my outburst. She looked up at me and said, "It's OK. I know now that I wasn't ruined."

I hugged her tightly. For a lifetime she had lived with these horrible words her mother had spoken. This false message of being responsible for my abuse threaded through my entire life.

Teen Jane stepped up and began talking to the small child in my lap. "Three, our mother was wrong when she told me I was like this since I was little. You were not ruined. And Nine?" she said adamantly, looking across at the child. "None of us were 'swinging doors'!"

Clearly angry, Teen Jane loved children and didn't want to see them hurt like this. Now every child, teen, young adult, and adult around the table was crying. All of me cried for the child who figured out how to survive the devastation that followed me from age three to twenty three.

As if it weren't enough to be abused, it had seemed that even the Bible judged me.

What the Storyteller and the Warrior Said

The Storyteller stopped crying and began to type on the laptop that appeared in front of her. This time, she and her warrior sister both typed. The words held more power when they typed together....

> *Finding myself condemned in the Bible was not at all helpful. Yet, it demonstrated how incorrect cultural beliefs influence us when interpreting the Bible. Jesus came to earth to show us how to live and care for the defenseless. He held the children and he respected women.*

He understood they were often blamed for the sins perpetrated upon them. He did not condemn them.

The twins stopped typing and read the piece aloud to the group. They all nodded their agreement. It was exactly what needed to be said. Jesus never wanted young girls (or boys) to be held responsible for the sins of adults.

The Young Adult Jane sat up straight and looked across at the seven year old holding the hammer. "I am so sorry I told you to board up the cave. You weren't created to do that. Daddy taught you how to use a hammer, and you loved building shelves to store memories. Your sister should not have needed to box up such awful memories."

While the various parts of me tried to care for each other, I reflected on how I had placed the boards on the outside of the cave to protect the world from me while taking on my abuser's shame as my own. I didn't need to be boarded up; someone needed to help me put up boards to keep *me* safe from the perpetrators. Without protection, once a child is abused, it will most likely happen again.

The Young Adult Jane stopped crying. She hugged the Sevens. Then she looked at me questioningly. "Why couldn't anyone ever help us?"

I understood exactly how she felt. I spoke to all the swollen red eyes looking to me for answers. "I am not sure why no one could help us. No one understood how desperately we needed help."

While listening to the conversations around the table, I heard "feelings" mentioned numerous times. This reminded me that we had not helped Nine with the feelings she was avoiding. She was still sitting next to Five, and they were the only two at the table not talking.

WHERE NINE AND FIVE TOOK US

The conversation with Five and Nine had been left unfinished during the tumult over the verse about "swinging doors." Now I walked over to sit beside them and said, "I'm sorry. I left you two just as you began to talk. Nine, you were telling Five you learned something from her. What was it?"

Nine had her arms crossed. Five looked at her then crossed her arms in the same way. I knew this look. Unless they uncrossed their arms, we would not get anywhere.

I didn't want assistance in solving this problem, but I welcomed support. Though my ability to communicate with my child selves had improved, this time I was unsure how to proceed.

Then Five whispered to Dr. Sue, "You didn't leave me."

Hugging Five, Dr. Sue confirmed that no, she hadn't left.

Nine listened to Five as she continued the story but did not uncross her arms.

We already knew the bad father forced Five to drink the beer then molested her, but there seemed to be more.

"Mother was there talking to the bad father. He was telling her that I had gone into the kitchen and helped myself to the beer. I didn't want to stay with the bad father. But after he told my mother that, I was afraid to go home with *her*. She pinched my arm with her fingernails and pulled me through the door. But I threw up on the porch."

"Oh no! You threw up! He lied about you sneaking to drink the beer. The beer made you sick!"

What a horrible predicament Five had been in, because my mother would have believed the bad father.

Both Nine and Five were watching me process this new information. They were proud of me for trusting my own memories. This memory could not have ended with my child self puking on her perpetrator's front porch. In other memories about throwing up, my mother blamed me and said I did it on purpose. This time, considering her anger about what the bad father told her, I could not imagine the situation ended well.

Five and Nine kept their arms crossed. They knew what happened, but the trauma hadn't been released yet. They had told the story without emotion.[2]

I wanted to help these child selves. I needed to step back and figure out what to do next. Our talk had not yet released the emotional material embedded in the trauma. Yes.... We would need to return to therapy.

"Thank you for telling me what happened, Five. You were in a fix. But Nine, you still haven't talked about your feelings or what you learned from Five."

She glared at me. She wasn't ready, either.

"Tell you what. Let's go ahead and eat. Everyone is hungry. As soon as you want to talk, I am ready to listen. And if you need help to process, we will ask for help—but I am the one who can always be here for you. Is this a good plan?"

They both nodded yes and pulled their chairs back to the table. The food Scott had prepared magically appeared and everyone, including Alice, began filling their plates with great anticipation.

As we ate, I thought back to how adamantly I, as an educator, often spoke about parents not taking everything at face value. There is always more to the story. But children don't have the capacity to put all the pieces together, let alone explain them.

---

2. Talk therapy methods used alone are less effective in treating trauma because it doesn't reach the deepest emotional material and internalized messages of shame connected to the traumatic memory stored in the Limbic brain.

The adult is responsible to trust the children and try to make sense of things. Even when children do something wrong, there is a reason behind their actions. My tendency to step into a random family's dramas to defend a child being blamed for something they didn't do, was an urge born on this horrible day.

Alice was watching me stare at my food.

"Do we need to change places?" she asked, no doubt alluding to how everyone kept moving around the table at the Mad Hatter's Tea Party.

I laughed. "This does remind me of all the chair switching at the tea party. But I will stay right here. Besides, I don't think you would want to give up your armchair!"

5
AFTER-DINNER THERAPY

The table was cleared, dishes washed, and my smallest child selves were tucked into bed. But Five and Nine, still with arms crossed, refused to go to bed. I motioned for them both to come to the office where Dr. Sue was waiting.

Alice seemed intent on dragging her armchair to the office. I could see no harm in this, since she had become part of the gathering and her presence seemed to comfort Five.

Five ran to Dr. Sue and exclaimed, "You didn't leave me!"

WHEN ADULTS LIE

Five began to cry. She still needed help. Nine and I watched as Five began to reprocess the entire memory with the help of EMDR. The details were the same, but there was more. I felt the Storyteller in me begin to explain what Five was emotionally and physically experiencing.

Mommy is here to pick me up. The bad father is telling her lies. He is telling her I went into the kitchen and drank beer. He is telling my mother he's sorry he left it where I could reach it. He didn't think I would drink it. He is telling her he shouldn't drink it, either. But he never thought a child would drink it. He told her I fell asleep and was mumbling something about being touched, but he didn't want to wake me. He sounds like he cares, and I almost believe him, but he is lying. My head hurts. My legs hardly hold me up. I am walking toward them.

Mommy's eyes are turning dark. She is going to shake me. No! I don't want her to do that! She is angry! She is believing the bad father! I am afraid! I want to stay with the bad father. I don't want to go with her! She believes his lies. I don't want to go out the door with her! I feel so sick. Her fingernails are digging into my arms. She is dragging me to the door. I am out of the door and ... Oh, no! I am throwing up! It is all over me. All over the porch. All over my mother's new shoes!

Nine was looking at Five with both sympathy and something akin to awe. I was speechless and very glad the memory hadn't caused me to throw up again. This child was going to be blamed for throwing up on purpose. The awful odor of regurgitated birthday cake and beer seemed to fill the office. I now understood why the very thought of beer had always been repugnant to me. It all made sense now.

But Five needed to tell more.

The bad father is telling mommy not to worry about the puke. He will clean it up. I hate him! I am sitting on the step. Mommy is in the car calling me. My legs won't stand up. She thinks I told the bad father about what happened to me when I was little. Why did he say that? I am stumbling to the car. She is driving fast around corners. I am throwing up again! It is all over the car and me!

When Children Lie

My heart sank. It just kept getting worse for Five. I felt her confusion as her mother yelled at her for throwing up again. I watched her walk in the front door and go into the bathroom and begin to pour water into the tub. Suddenly, she was in a different bathtub. She was smaller. On that day, her mother told her she was dirty. On this day, she said she was disgusting.

I am in the bathtub. Daddy is home. I can hear them talking. She is angry. He sounds tired. Now she is in the bathroom. She is holding a trash bag. Her new shoes are in it. She is telling me to throw my dress in the bag. I am out of the tub. I am dressed. Daddy is coming to talk to me. I need to decide what to do. I can tell the truth, but it won't matter, and it may make things worse. I might need to lie.

I felt myself walk to my bedroom where I continued to see the scene play out in my mind. My father looked tired. He was sad as he sat beside my child self on the bed.

"Jeannie, did you drink from the glass on the counter?"

Well, I did. So I answered, "Yes."

"Why did you do that?"

I had no answer to this, so I shrugged.

"Did you learn you shouldn't drink things left on counters?"

Well, I already knew that, so I responded, "Yes."

Then he said, "You know you ruined your mother's new shoes when you threw up."

This was also true, so I nodded yes.

"You need to tell your mother you're sorry."

Now, this was a problem. I felt the child inside me experiencing the emotion-laden decision she needed to make. She looked this way, then that way. She scrunched up her little face and then she sat up straight and said, "I can't do that."

How Five Was Strong

My father looked exhausted as he walked out of my bedroom. Five wanted to run after him and explain, but she knew it wouldn't help. She hadn't done anything wrong, but telling the truth would only make things worse. She could hear her parents talking and felt her mother's anger.

"What is wrong with her? Why won't she just say she is sorry for what she did?"

"I don't know, but she isn't going to," he said.

Five heard the front door shut as her father left. Her heart sank as the car started. He was leaving her alone with her mother. She braced herself.

> *The door is opening. Mommy is standing in the doorway. She is very angry.*
>
> *I am screaming, "Get out of my room! Get out!"*
>
> *"Say you are sorry! You know what you did, and you ruined my shoes! Say you are sorry!"*
>
> *Her nails dug into my arms as my body flailed back and forth. On the outside, my body was limp and flailing from the shaking, but inside I was strong.*

Feeling the couch beneath me, I looked at Dr. Sue and began explaining. "I was never going to say it. They could have taken me to a field and dragged me behind wild horses. They could have sent me in front of a firing squad. I was never going to say a lie against myself."

I knew this was my true "self." I felt the same strength inside her that had enabled me to survive. She learned adults could lie and she could lie about what adults did to her. My little five-year-old self couldn't control anything in her world, but she could control the words coming out of her mouth. No one could force her to say she was sorry for something she didn't do. Not even her love for her father could make her cross that line.

I continued to process. "This is the part of me who finally

told the truth and decided to publish *BRAVE*. This is who I am. I finally found me."

The Long-Term Consequences

What a terrible situation for a small child. Five couldn't win. No matter what direction she went, it wasn't going to turn out well.

Five, who had been listening, began talking again.

> *My daddy is home. I am telling him Mommy shook me. I am showing him my arms, the red and where her nails dug into me. He is sad. He is telling me he doesn't know why she shakes me, but he needs me to be good and try not to make her upset. My daddy needs me to help him. I can't tell Mommy I am sorry, but I can try to be good. This means I need to stop crying. She doesn't like it when I cry. I can't cry.*

Once again, my father faced a situation in which he felt he needed to ask me to be the "adult." My only choice was to take on that responsibility.

> *I can't cry, I don't want to be sad again. I want to go to parties and run in the field behind our new house. I don't know why bad men keep hurting me, but I want to be happy.*

My mind was busy processing. This made complete sense. I felt all the pain and turmoil inside me. No one was going to believe me. The only one who would believe me was me. I would not say sorry for something I didn't do! If I let the rage and terror inside me walk around in the world, I would not be able to help my father. Somehow, I needed to set aside what happened and go back to the happy little girl who went to the party.

In a therapy session much earlier in the journey, I had sensed myself splitting the "good" emotions and feelings from the "bad" ones. That emotional turmoil was an exact match to this day. When Five split for the first time and became the One Who Cries and the One Who Lives, it enabled me to be that happy little girl again.

No matter what happened to me, I would have what I came to call "my internal compass" to guide me. Deep inside I knew what I would and would not do to survive. I would always stay true to myself.

I am proud of my father for not forcing me to apologize. It is doubtful that any of this made sense to him. Without an understanding of the effects of trauma, my behavior was often inexplicable. This was just one more day of confusing behavior.

∾

We sat in the office for some time considering what we now understood. Five had accomplished some intense processing, and now she looked exhausted. She asked Dr. Sue for one more hug. Then she opened the door and said, "You can leave now. But I understand you aren't *really* leaving me."

They smiled at each other. Five said goodnight and walked down a long hallway to climb into bed. I followed, kissed her on the forehead, and sat beside her as she drifted off into the peaceful sleep of a child who was brave and strong and now had adults in her life who believed her—and were never going to leave.

Alice joined me, dragging her armchair down the hallway. She curled up in the chair and informed me she would sleep beside Five. I left them together and closed the door. Tomorrow would be another day.

6
CAMPFIRE REFLECTIONS

The following evening, everyone decided to gather round a campfire and continue talking. The difficulties children face in the adult world, sometimes decimate the natural process of sense making. This was never any clearer than in the confusing and traumatic story Five had begun to tell at the dinner table and finished later in the office. The tangle of confusion in her mind as she tried to figure out what to do was reminiscent of Alice's quandaries after she fell down the rabbit hole while chasing the White Rabbit.

Looking now at Alice and Five sitting beside each other near the fire, I realized how much they had in common. I always enjoyed how Alice explained much of her thinking in *Alice in Wonderland*. We seldom give children credit for the serious thought they put into their choices. We often consider choices impulsive and do not reflect on what they may have been thinking.

During EMDR processing, I was often amazed at the logic involved in the choices made by my child selves. I don't think this was evident to my parents. A bit more probing on my father's part might have proven profitable; but the pressure my mother put on him to press for an apology was intense.

FIVE TALKS TO ALICE ABOUT BEING SMALL

Alice had dragged her armchair to the campfire circle. The chair looked odd sitting amongst the logs, but Alice did appear decidedly more comfortable than the others. She and Five began talking.

"Alice, you know when you went to the White Rabbit's house to find the gloves and fan?"

Alice nodded yes, and looked curiously at the small child who seemed to know all about her adventures in Wonderland.

Five continued, "I think my daddy believed I drank what was in the glass like you did. You were curious about the bottle, weren't you?"

Alice knew her own story well and quoted the part Five was describing:

> *'I know SOMETHING interesting is sure to happen,'*
> *she said to herself, 'whenever I eat or drink anything; so,*
> *I'll just see what this bottle does. I do hope it'll make me*
> *grow large again, for really I'm quite tired of being such*
> *a tiny little thing!'*
>
> –Alice

"But Five, I should not have done that! What a bad idea. I was tired of being so little, but I grew up way too fast."

Five could relate to growing up too fast. "I was tired of being little, too! I couldn't stop them from hurting me, but I didn't want to drink what was on the counter. I'm sad my daddy never knew I didn't want to drink it."

Alice looked at Five sympathetically. "But you told him you did drink it. Why? It wasn't exactly a lie, but it wasn't the truth, either. Didn't that make things worse? Wouldn't he have believed you?"

Five was quiet as she considered how to answer this question. That was really the problem, wasn't it? Adults believed children told lies; and therefore when other adults told their version of the story, but were lying, who was going to believe the child?

Five began slowly. "Well, I was trying to think very hard, but my head hurt and after I threw up, there was no question about whether I drank the beer or not. Kind of like when you got really big in the White Rabbit's house. Everyone knew what you did."

Now Alice was thinking. "Yes, it was certain you did drink it. So, you didn't lie. You told your dad the truth."

"Exactly," Five said. "If I would have told them the bad father made me drink the beer, it would have looked like I was trying to blame someone else. It would have been like you saying the White Rabbit made you drink it. No one would have believed you."

"Well," Alice pondered. "In my case it would have been a lie, but in your case it was true. But I agree; no one was going to believe a child and say the bad father was lying. But children do lie sometimes, you know."

Jane, who had been listening, stepped in to talk to the two girls. "Remember what we learned? Misunderstood behavior is often based on unmet needs. Five, what were you needing when Daddy came in to talk to you?"

Five considered the question for a minute. "It is kind of like asking what was I feeling, right? Bad things happened to me again and I needed Daddy to care about me, but if he thought I was lying about drinking the beer, then he would think I was lying about bad things happening and that would really make it all worse, wouldn't it?"

There was a murmur around the campfire. Her logic was truly remarkable for being so young. If she wanted someone to care, then she needed to seem like she was being honest and knew she had done something wrong. If she tried to tell them what happened, then it would look like she was trying to blame the bad father for what she did. No one would care about her if they thought she was lying.

Alice sighed, looked at Five compassionately, and said, "It was really way too complicated for such a young child to have to figure out. You were doing the best you could."

Refusing To Apologize

"Thank you, Alice. I thought you would understand. You got into some confusing things yourself. But I am sad because my daddy lived his whole life thinking I did a naughty thing, then refused to say I was sorry."

Seeing how sad this made Jeannie, Alice said, "But you couldn't apologize for something you didn't do."

Five was crying. Jane picked her up and asked, "What would you tell him if he were here now?"

This was almost too much for Five. She missed her daddy so much. He left when she wasn't there. Even if she wanted to talk to him about this, she couldn't.

Five began to talk through her sobs, "Daddy! Why did you leave me? I wanted to tell you I didn't want to drink what was in the glass. That bad father made me drink it. I was afraid. Everyone left me there with him. I was little. I had to do what he told me. Then he touched me and I couldn't stop him. I felt so sick. He told good lies. I didn't think anyone would believe this happened to me again. I would be blamed for wanting attention. What could I do?"

The One Who Cries handed out tissues around the circle.

Five continued, "Daddy, I didn't know what to do, but it wasn't my fault I threw up. I never threw up on purpose. She wanted me to say I was sorry, but I didn't throw up on purpose or go in and drink the beer by myself. You didn't make me apologize!"

Knowing her father hadn't forced her to apologize seemed

to help her for a minute, but then the sobs broke out again.

"I wanted you to know I was doing my best to be a good girl! I tried to be good my whole life. I couldn't ever tell you what happened to me, because no one would believe me, and I wanted you to believe I was a good girl. I *was* a good girl! I couldn't apologize and look like a bad girl when I knew I was a good girl."

Jane held her closer. "Yes, you were a good girl, and very brave! You made the only choice you could make. I am sure it didn't make any sense to Daddy and he wasn't ever going to make you apologize. You both got caught in the web of confusion together. He still knew who you were. He knew you were brave and strong."

Non Janyne was listening. "The problem is the secrets adults keep, the lies they tell, and children who get caught in the middle. Children have no power and they make the best choices they can; but telling the truth is often a path that doesn't seem safe. They either learn to lie from the adults or are placed in situations where lying is their only choice."

God Understood

Jane, who had been listening to Non Janyne, blurted out, "God tried to tell us he understood!"

All eyes turned toward her.

"Remember during the second year of therapy? Our friend Lori sent us a verse. We had problems with verses. We weren't sure we wanted a verse."

The room shuddered, thinking about the Song of Solomon verse, but Nine knew what verse Jane was talking about.

"Yes, it was when I was beginning to understand what happened wasn't my fault! I kept that verse! Let me go get it!"

Nine ran to the house, then returned with a piece of paper

with the verse printed on it, and began reading. Looking over her shoulder, I saw she had underlined several parts.

> *He sent from on high, he took me; he drew me out of many waters. <u>He rescued me from my strong enemy</u> and from those who hated me, <u>for they were too mighty for me.</u> They confronted me in the day of my calamity, but the Lord was my support. He brought me out into a broad place; <u>he rescued me, because he delighted in me.</u> The Lord dealt with me according to my <u>righteousness; according to the cleanness of my hands he rewarded me.</u> For I have kept the ways of the Lord, and have not wickedly departed from my God. For all his rules were before me, and his statutes I didn't put away from me. <u>I was blameless before him, and I kept myself from my guilt.</u> So, the Lord has rewarded me according to my righteousness, according to the cleanness of my hands in his sight* (Psalm 18:16-24, ESV).

The Young Adult Jane looked around the campfire as the scripture words sank in. "I don't remember this verse. Maybe I wasn't there the day we got it? This is so much better than the other one."

Nine looked triumphant. Five looked up at Jane and said, "God understood why I wouldn't say I was sorry. I couldn't say it, because I didn't do anything wrong."

LEARNING TO LIE

The evening was growing late and everyone was staring at the dying campfire embers. I thought surely this emotional breakthrough would end the evening, but Nine was still considering Non Janyne's thoughts about how children learn to lie.

"I learned to lie from the bad father. What you do is include just enough truth, sound very sincere and convincing, and make sure the truth seems like the lie. I didn't like to lie, but sometimes it was the only way to stay safe. He told those lies so he would stay safe, and I learned to do the same. Maybe he learned to lie when he was little."

Jane looked at Nine. "So Five didn't lie, but you still learned to lie from what happened? Why did you believe you needed to lie?"

"Sometimes it was because no one would believe me. Telling the truth usually made things worse. Even if they believed me, no one was going to do anything to the bad person, and I would get in trouble for wanting attention. Sometimes the lies were because my mother was going to make a really big deal about something that wasn't a big deal at all."

Everyone seemed to have an example of a similar situation. After they told their stories, Jane asked, "What would have made this different? What did we need?"

Eight's answer was immediate. "We needed to be trusted. We needed to know if we told the truth about what happened, we would be believed."

Heads all nodded "yes" around the circle as Eight continued. "There were some things that probably caused Mother to not trust us. As much as we want to think she didn't have reasons to not trust us, there were times when we were kind of confusing."

Eight was right. Many times, while processing a childhood memory during EMDR, my adult mind enabled me to see things from an adult perspective. It didn't change what happened, but it did help me appreciate my parents' inability to understand my trauma-related behaviors. There were some valid reasons they believed I told lies.

The Easter story Eight would eventually tell was important because it explained so much about my behavior. For now, the hour was late, Alice was sound asleep in her comfy armchair, and the others decided their beds would be more comfortable than the hard logs on which they had been sitting.

Part II
WHAT MY CHILD SELVES LEARNED

The story of Five, saved for this book, serves as a foundation for Part II. On the surface, it seems Five's story was about an unpredictable child who drank beer, revealed family secrets in a drunken stupor, then refused to apologize for throwing up on, and ruining, her mother's new shoes.

Five's story is an example of how children's behaviors are so easily misunderstood. Like many days in the lives of families, what appeared to be happening on the surface was far from what I was actually experiencing.

While reflecting on Five's memories, Dr. Sue and I wondered: If my mother had taken me to the car and asked what happened or asked if I was afraid to talk in front of the bad father—would I have told the truth?

I responded, "Well, that would have required me to be living an entirely different life, wouldn't it?"

We agreed. What happened was part of my cultural context. This included obeying adults, controlling my behavior, and keeping family secrets. There was nothing in this context that would have helped my parents understand my behavior.

Without understanding unmet attachment needs and their effects on my development and behavior, my desperate attempts to "be a good girl" fell in a wasteland of relationship with my mother. When controlling behavior is the focus, it is difficult to consider the unmet needs underlying a child's actions.

Children can make sense to us, but it isn't always easy.

Sometimes they cross their arms and refuse to talk. This can happen even in the best of relationships. Will we believe them? Will we listen? Will we care? In trusting relationships, they will eventually talk. And then we need to listen carefully. Their perception of what happened may not be fully correct, but it is their truth. They need us to care deeply.

The only way to help children is to understand the effects of their experiences. It often isn't possible to know what happened to them, but my hope is that telling Jeannie's stories will help us look underneath children's behaviors and see the unmet needs.

In Part II, my child selves return to the campfire. Alice, who now felt like family, is always sitting in her armchair. Though "Dr. Sue" is not present at the campfire, she is involved in the telling of the stories that began as part of therapy. Often, while storytelling, someone says something that sounds much like her. Just as children in healthy relationships internalize their mothers, I began to internalize the care of my therapist in the process of becoming enough for myself.

7
ATTACHMENT AND THE "MOTHER"

The story told in *BRAVE* provides a complete overview of my insecure attachment with my mother. Attachment is at the core of both emotional growth and brain development in early childhood. It is also the foundation for building healthy relationships. Disrupted attachment is part of why the internalized messages embedded with my trauma were so difficult for me to process. There is not much in my mental health/illness story that wasn't, at least partially, due to unmet attachment needs.

I could have recovered from what happened the day of the party, but it would have required a mother who truly knew who I was and what I would and would not choose to do. Knowing me, delighting in me, and trusting me from the moment I was born would have changed everything. Unmet attachment needs haunted me for a lifetime.

ALICE AND FIVE NEED A MOTHER

Everyone had gathered around the campfire again, and Alice and Five were deep into a discussion.

"Alice, your book never talks about your parents," said Five. "You never seemed to have a mother. Did you have a mother?"

Alice looked almost surprised at the question. "No, I guess I was strong enough to not need a mother. I seemed to be the one taking care of myself and everyone else."

Five thought about this for a minute before she said, "Well, the one mother in Wonderland, the Duchess, wasn't a very good mother. Maybe you were better off without a mother. In my case they always seemed to walk away."

Alice looked at her sadly. "No, you didn't have good luck with mothers. But I think having mothers is important."

"Me too," said Five. "Everyone needs someone to care about them—like a mother."

Alice hugged Five. "I am glad Dr. Sue cared about you."

Yes, Dr. Sue could model the nurturing I missed as a child; but I was the only one who could permanently become enough for myself. To work toward this goal, it was necessary to reflect on how disrupted attachment affected my development. It had a lot to do with the culture of my childhood.

AN INFANT'S FIRST EXPERIENCES

Medical practices during the generation in which I was born were a partial reason for my mother not bonding with me. Unconscious during my birth, she (by her own admission) left my care to the nurses during the first five days of my life. For those of us who study attachment, these practices are appalling—yet they were standard at the time.

One day, while discussing how children adopted at birth often experience attachment issues, I said, "We come out of the womb desperately needing to find the one with whom we bonded in-utero." Attachment begins before birth and the child is ready and seeking to bond with the mother. When there are complications or inadequate opportunity for bonding, it is imperative for the child to have experiences designed to repair this disruption. If we are intentional about it, repair can happen.

Attachment repair didn't occur after my first five days in the hospital. During EMDR, my earliest memories were in the crib with adults and brothers wandering through the room. This was not atypical, but being held or hugged by my mother was never part of my memories—at any age (though pictures did show me being held for family photos).

Research has shown the mother's gaze while holding an infant, is essential in helping the child learn emotional regulation and soothing.[1] The science of neurobiology is now documenting what D. W. Winnicott sensed about the importance of the mother's gaze:

> *The mother gazes at the baby in her arms, and the baby gazes at his mother's face and finds himself therein...*

> –D. W. Winnicott

I can't help but wonder if birthing procedures and child-rearing practices may be partially to blame for the high incidence of anxiety and depression plaguing the adults of my generation. There are, of course, stress and genetic factors. But when I found the source of my anxiety, it was rooted in childhood experiences with my mother that lacked relationship.

We don't become anxious adults without a cause. If you listen to the descriptions of anxiety given by adults, you can hear the similarity between those descriptions and the anxiousness of a small child who needs an adult to help her soothe.

A difficult task during therapy was learning to soothe myself between appointments. As my dissociative mechanisms for surviving became less effective, it was evident I did not learn to self soothe as a child.

The ability to self soothe develops in the neurobiology of the attachment relationship. "The kinds of communicative signals that are strong releasers of oxytocin are mutual gaze, certain tones of voice that are similar to child-directed speech or 'motherese,' and certain qualities of touch."[2]

---

1. For recent research on the neurobiology of attachment I recommend: Baylin, J. and D. A. Hughes, *The Neurobiology of Attachment-Focused Therapy* (New York: W. W. Norton & Co., 2016)

2. ibid (p. 101)

THE NEED FOR ENGAGEMENT AND ATTENTION

The young child's most critical need, beyond physical safety, is the need to be seen. A baby's face is designed to engage with the adults. It is hard to look at a baby without going into some form of babbling. This is exactly what the new human needs. When mothers do not engage with the young child (see videos of the Still Face Experiment), it places the child in great distress. In my memories, my infant self could not elicit an expression of engagement or delight from my mother.

During the first half of the 20th century much (but not all) parenting resources admonished mothers to not spoil infants, to keep them on a schedule, and not pick them up when they cried—because they just wanted attention. (Exactly!) There was very little understanding about attachment.

In his 1928 book, *The Psychological Care of Infant and Child*,[3] J.B. Watson advised,

> *Never hug and kiss [your children], never let them sit on your lap. If you must, kiss them once on the forehead when they say goodnight…. In a week's time, you will find how easy it is to be perfectly objective with your child and at the same time kindly. You will be utterly ashamed at the mawkish, sentimental way you have been handling it.*

Watson was both applauded and criticized for his views on child rearing and, at the end of his life, regretted some of what he had said; but it is certain that he was highly influential in the ways in which children were raised in the mid 1900s.[4] I

---

3. Watson, J. B., *The Psychological Care of Infant and Child* (London: Allen, 1928).

4. For a full analysis of J.B. Watson's views in comparison to other advice of the day, see: Bigelow, K. M., & Morris, E. K., "John B. Watson's Advice on Child Rearing: Some Historical Context," *Behavioral Development Bulletin* 10, no. 1 (2016): 26-30. Retrieved from http://psycnet.apa.org/fulltext/ 2014-55587-006.html. http://psycnet.apa.org/fulltext/

can see this influence in my parents' childrearing practices.

My mother was college educated and would have been aware of the information touted as "best practices" for child rearing. The well-educated were most susceptible to these influences. Some of these practices still linger and I see the present child-rearing generation struggling to find the balance amidst the wide range of viewpoints expressed on their phones and computers. My best advice is, if the source doesn't mention attachment, set it aside and find another source that does. If you understand attachment, the choices will be much easier to make.

The "Good Enough Mother"

D.W. Winnicott coined the phrase, "good enough mother" in his book, *Playing and Reality*.[5] An important aspect of this mother was that her entire devotion to the infant slowly tapered in a way that increased the child's ability to self soothe and regulate. This secure foundation of met needs via a devoted relationship allows the child to successfully navigate future frustrations.

Winnicott's work, published in 1971, is in stark contrast to Behaviorism which told mothers to train infants to be on *their* schedule. Being a "good enough mother," as described by Winnicott, is simply good mothering—not some form of "perfect" mothering in which the parent feels in control of the child.

A Mother and Her Child

My parents' generation valued compliant children. I was precocious and strong willed. The 1950s culture didn't always view small, independent girls in a positive light. As a pastor's wife with one child already prone to troublesome behavior, my

---

5. Winnicott, D.W., *Playing and Reality* (London: Routledge, 1971).

mother would have felt great pressure to control me and would have been frustrated by the effort.

Without a securely-attached relationship, the chances of my mother and me living in peace with each other were minimal. When the abuse occurred at three, our already fragile relationship provided no safe space for healing. The importance of secure attachment in dealing with the adverse experiences of childhood cannot be overemphasized (see Addendum III: ACE Study).

If my mother had understood being a "good enough mother" was a matter of relationship and not control, if she had been raised in a home where she had received the nurturing she needed, rather than experiencing some form of childhood trauma (which I believe she did),[6] my young self would not have suffered the psychological damage described in *BRAVE*.

When a mother is unable to heal her own story, she cannot be the mother her child needs. I do not believe my mother intended to hurt me so severely. Considering her social context, she probably believed she was being a good mother. In many ways, she was; but she wasn't what Winnicott described as a "good enough mother." Relational care and attention would have changed my life.

Unmet Attachment Needs and Neediness

My need for attention had tragic consequences. The shame that developed around seeking attention wound throughout my life. Getting attention and fearing attention caused an internal war, and I was the loser. The only possible way to heal

---

6. Physiological effects of childhood abuse across generations, see: Gray, S.A.O., Jones, C.W., Theall, K.P., Glackin, E., & Drury, S.S., "Thinking Across Generations: Unique Contributions of Maternal Early Life and Prenatal Stress to Infant Physiology," *Journal of the American Academy of Child and Adolescent Psychiatry* (2017). Retrieved from https://www.ncbi.nlm.nih.gov/pubmed/29096774

my need for attention was to receive attention.

A child can only grow to be independent if allowed to be dependent. The child who suffers from a lack of attention needs attention, but if trauma is involved, they may reject it at the same time (especially attention from the primary caregiver in foster/adoption settings).[7]

Independent children are those who have experienced a "good enough" relationship. Behavior management methods designed to teach students to be independent are misdirected. There is no greater drive in children than the desire to be independent. From the moment children say, "I can do it myself!" they are seeking the day when they can do everything on their own. Children become overly dependent because they have not experienced complete dependence on one human totally committed to their care.

I was the child who followed teachers around. I needed attention. Children who feel safe want to be independent. The more a teacher allowed me to need her, the less I needed her. The more a teacher tried to distance herself, the more I needed her. (This gets complicated with extreme attachment trauma usually identified as RAD. I discuss this further in Chapter 17. In all cases, the teacher must understand his or her role as a caring professional, with strong boundaries, whose focus is instruction.)[8]

---

7. Addendum III provides additional insights to the working with the most severe needs of many adopted/foster children who have experienced disrupted attachment and trauma.

8. While not addressing underlying causes, this article provides an overview of appropriate RAD strategies in the classroom: Williams, K., "For Teachers of Children Experiencing the Effects of Early Trauma" (September 24, 2018). Retrieved from https://www.instituteforattachment.org/for-teachers-of-children-experiencing-the-effects-of-early-trauma/

Reflecting on Attachment

One profound aspect of my healing involved coming to terms with my unmet attachment needs. My attachment woundings were pre-verbal and difficult to distinguish from personality. They exhibited as a needy personality, but this was not "me." The unmet need to attach to a mother figure drove my behavior for over sixty years.

The issues entrenched in the "me" who showed up in therapy five years after my mother's death were a result of disrupted attachment, trauma, generational patterns, and a mother who desperately needed healing. My "neediness" wasn't me. It was what happened to me.

One time I had a conversation with a grandfather who had recently received custody of his granddaughters. He said, "It is good that they were so little. They won't remember what happened." Having come to realize how my earliest pre-verbal experiences had affected me, I tried to explain to him why this common misconception is incorrect. I encouraged him to seek therapy for the girls.

What occurs during the earliest months of life is the foundation for relationships, how we handle adverse experiences, and the ability to achieve the critical balance for mental health. My unmet attachment needs appear in every childhood experience included in the following chapters.

තු

Sighing loudly, I looked up from my laptop computer and realized everyone had gone to bed—except Alice, who had fallen asleep in her armchair. I covered her with a blanket, kissed her on the forehead, and looked up at the moonlit night sky. "Goodnight, Moon," I whispered. "Tomorrow is another chapter."

8
TRAUMA NEEDS A "MOTHER"

Trauma is not what happens to us, but what we hold inside in the absence of an empathetic witness.

–Peter A. Levine

The attachment relationship developed in infancy is foundational to helping the young child navigate during the early childhood years (toddler to early elementary). This is true in happy childhoods and crucial in childhoods filled with adverse experiences. Sadly, the mother figure is often part of the problem.

As I typed the above paragraph, Alice, who had awakened in her armchair by the campfire and was surprised to find herself there, began dragging the chair into the kitchen to watch me type.

"Well, the Duchess was certainly part of the problem!" Alice declared. "She sang that horrible song to her baby. Poor little thing."

> *Speak roughly to your little boy,*
> *And beat him when he sneezes:*
> *He only does it to annoy,*
> *Because he knows it teases.*

> –Alice

Now Five was listening. "What an awful song! That's like blaming me for throwing up and crying. I didn't *want* to bother my mother!"

"No," said Alice. "You were trying to be a good girl."

Releasing Trauma

After the abuse at three, I desperately needed a mother's care, but my outward releasing of trauma was met with extreme disapproval. When I most needed her help, my mother was unable to provide it.

During EMDR, I witnessed what the release of trauma looks and sounds like. There is not much about releasing trauma that is "socially acceptable." While healing, I shook, I cried, sat in bed and stared, vomited, threw things, and yelled. It was often explosive, but so indispensable for healing!

Where is it OK for a child (or adult) to release emotions and feelings; especially when trauma-induced? When is it alright for a child to scream? How does a child release the very real physical energy of trauma?

It is crucial for adults to calmly receive the child's anger—even if directed at them. I understand this is challenging!

At one point early in therapy, I found myself wandering around my condo tearing paper into tiny of pieces and filling multiple wastebaskets. It was imperative to do something physical in order to release the trauma surfacing in therapy. It needed to be a physical release. I spent days obsessively tearing paper.

Tearing paper was an adult version of what I tried to do as a child. It was mild compared to my child self's release. At three, my release of trauma looked much like a tantrum. I needed a relationship with my mother that would have allowed me to release the trauma. Instead, it was held in my body for sixty years!

Healing Trauma With Attachment

Attachment wounding and trauma were wound tightly

together in my being. Again and again, my three-year-old self surfaced with additional trauma. What unimaginable damage had been done to a small child in the span of a few days!

The deepest healing involved a memory that took place after the abuse—during several tumultuous days of painful interactions with my mother. During EMDR, I saw this child self in the bedroom stacking her ABC blocks.

> *"They won't stay up! They keep falling down!"*
> *I could feel how desperate she was to stack the blocks.*
> *She trembled so from the trauma, that she kept knocking*
> *them down. She tried again and again, becoming more*
> *and more desperate with each attempt.*

I opened my eyes. "It feels like I might die if I can't stack them. The man helped me stack them, and then he hurt me. It feels like my life depends on stacking the blocks *by myself!*"

I wanted to stop. I could feel my rage growing as the blocks kept falling. I couldn't leave this child self there like that. I had to process the memory. I closed my eyes again as the memory continued to surface. I felt the child knock the blocks across the floor and then pick up the ones closest to her, and begin to throw them.

> *I hear my mommy's heels clip-clopping on the wooden*
> *floor! Closer and closer ... Pick up the blocks!*
> *The door is opening! "You were throwing the blocks*
> *again, weren't you?"*
> *"No, no!" I am screaming.*
> *She is coming toward me. Shaking! She is shaking me!*
> *"No, no!"*

The sensation of being shaken was familiar by this point of therapy. My body flailed as I cried, remembering. Then I saw my mother lean over to pick up the blocks and felt my small body lunge at her, knocking her down, while I kicked and grabbed at the blocks. My mother scrambled to her feet and rushed through the door.

Delving more deeply into the memory, I became the child sitting on the floor with the blocks and felt the pain deep inside me begin to engulf my body. The adult me knew the pain. Deep in my abdomen, the pain was part of me all my life. Then I began yelling at Dr. Sue.

> *"You made me feel the pain. You told me I would get better if I felt the pain. It hurts inside me! I am not better. Why did you make me feel? I didn't want to feel anything. You told me I would be better! I am not better!"*

I could hear Dr. Sue affirming my anger. She understood. Her calm voice held me as unimaginable waves of pain poured over me. I could hear myself screaming. I was drowning in the pain. I needed the only person who ever understood my pain to help me.

Then I heard a child's voice cry from within me: "Please hug me! I need you to hug me."

As Dr. Sue embraced me, it was as if this part of me had never been held before. It was the deep core pain of a little girl who was rejected because she yelled at her mother. But this time, there was no rejection.

I tried to control this violent anger my entire life. I feared it. I hated it. I believed it would destroy me and those closest to me. The only way to heal, though, was to release the anger—without subsequently being rejected.

Dr. Sue remained decidedly calm and accepting. It was the type of care I had always needed. I needed a "mother" to demonstrate: "Even in the face of your most violent anger, I am here. I see you, I know you, I care about you. Your anger can never make me walk away."

This calm acceptance in the face of my anger healed my child self, who believed no one could ever love her if the anger exploded out of her. I felt complete acceptance as I left the office.

This was the experience my child self had needed immediately after the abuse. When that did not occur, it added another layer onto my unmet attachment needs. The damage to my relationship with my mother was present in every subsequent interaction.

INTERNALIZING TRAUMA

Because I was unable to release the trauma, the next step was depression. What could not be released outwardly, was internalized and would haunt me for a lifetime. During an EMDR session, I found my four-year-old self wandering aimlessly through my childhood home with no will to engage. Later in therapy, I made the connection between Four and the adult depression of Non Janyne.

The inability to express trauma becomes silence. The inability to process emotions or feelings becomes deadness. The inner tension becomes unreleased restless energy that cannot be soothed. The avoidance of everything internal becomes anxiety. The lack of emotional relationship during this dark time in my childhood caused me to wander through the house; and as an adult I would sit in a chair and stare at nothing.

Undoubtedly, my withdrawal at four was much easier for my mother than was my explosive behavior at three. What my three-year-old self learned was, no matter how hard she tried to have her desperate needs met, it wasn't going to happen. Depression is the death of hope.

Sadly, depression was a generational pattern. Over her lifetime, my mother consistently suffered from depression and anxiety. Her own mother was ill for many years and died when my mother was in her early twenties. This leads me to believe my mother probably never had her own needs met as a child.

Most of my memories of my mother were of a distant person who never looked at me directly unless she was angry. She was as lost as her small child. She most likely had no foundation upon which to be a mother. She and I wandered around the house together, but did not interact in meaningful ways.

Before therapy, I believed my depression to be genetic. When I found my four-year-old self wandering in the dark house and researched childhood depression, I knew this wasn't true (further explained in Chapter 9). I am not sure Five could have pulled herself out of this darkness without moving to a different house. Sometimes a change in location does help; possibly because it removes environmental triggers. Maybe my mother hoped for this during our many moves.

FIVE FIGURES OUT HOW TO BE INVISIBLE

We moved about the time I turned five. Before Five talked about the party, she took us on a tour of her new neighborhood.

This neighborhood was more isolated from major intersections, and there were lots of children roaming around. My parents probably felt I would be safe among all the children. The dark house was left behind. It was now possible for me to be independent; and in my case, independence meant freedom from my mother's constant control. This made my life an odd mixture of tight control and complete freedom.

There were several memories of me hiding under the dining room table in this new house. I felt invisible because my mother never interacted with me there. A treasured picture shows me sitting under the table with an accordion—and a decidedly unhappy expression. I processed this memory twice with EMDR before I understood its significance.

An evangelist occasionally stayed at our house. He was a gentle and kind man who played the saw (sounds like a violin). I gladly gave up my bedroom when he came, because I was absolutely fascinated with his saw playing!

One day, he was packing the saw in his suitcase when he saw me standing in the doorway. He smiled and said the saw was too dangerous to play, but would I like to try the accordion? Yes! But I didn't want to get in trouble for trying to get attention, so I asked if I could take it under the table—because I was invisible there.

He looked amused, but went along with my plan. When my father came home and spotted me under the table with an accordion, he went to get the camera. This presented a problem because, when they developed the film, my mother would know. I finally understood what the expression on my face in the photo was about—I was looking that way because I had asked for attention! And taking a picture would ruin everything, because I would no longer be invisible.

What began as a negative—my mother not "seeing" me in the dark house—turned into a positive because I figured out how to be invisible in the new house. This was often a good thing. My life was easier when invisible.

My mother and I could have learned to coexist. But something about her inability to control me triggered her anger. If this hadn't been the case, I might have been willing to be "visible."

Lack of attachment is not the same as physical abuse.

Six and the Mother Doll

The prop I came to know as the Mother Doll, had been

sitting in a corner of the therapy office since my first appointment. The doll was about ten inches high, with a pink polka dot elongated star-shaped body and two yellow yarn pigtails. She had small glittery pompom "buttons" on her stomach and her mouth was a circle of glitter. To top off her odd appearance, she sported a bead necklace that identified her as "Nellie."[1]

Honestly, I wondered why such a strange doll was sitting in the corner next to a large "doctor" bear. Since Dr. Sue sublet the office from another therapist, it was just something to ignore. It was a relief to know she hadn't chosen it. Nellie was an odd little doll.

One day, Six was working on mother issues, when Dr. Sue got up from her chair and picked up the doll. She looked at the doll a second, then set her in the chair. The intent was for me to speak to the Mother Doll, but instead I began to cry—no, I sobbed and cried uncontrollably.

"It's her eyebrow!"

No memory of therapy brings us more amusement than this now-resolved memory. What a reaction! It wasn't possible for me to even look at the doll, and the tears wouldn't stop.

Dr. Sue simply said, repeating my words, "The eyebrow." And she waited.

Slowly, getting my adult self grounded back on the couch, I remembered one of my mother's eyebrows arched much higher than the other—exactly like the doll. I went home and searched for a picture to demonstrate this, and uploaded it to my phone to take to the next therapy session. There was nothing else about the doll that even remotely reminded me of my mother who was always stylish and well coifed.

---

1. Pictures of objects and people in my story, including one of Nellie, are available at my website: https://www.janyne.org/

If there was ever a question about my childhood trauma including my relationship with my mother, my passionate reaction to the Mother Doll was enough to convince me. There was nothing in my carefully-constructed, pre-therapy childhood story that would have predicted such an explosive response.

My reaction to the Mother Doll made more sense after the memories of my mother shaking me surfaced. Accepting that my mother hurt me—not only emotionally, but physically abused me in this way—was difficult. When Five finally told her story, she identified a look in her mother's eye when she was going to shake her. This was the look I saw on the Mother Doll's face. It was the eyebrow.

When Trauma Has No "Mother"

I remember listening to my college students talk about missing their mothers. I wondered what that would feel like and could never understand why I felt no attachment to my own mother. I lived out this series of interactions through avoidance and anxiety. There was no place in my life to express the fact my mother had never been the "mother" I desperately needed. Sadly, her very presence in the room was fraught with anxiety for me.

Looking up from my laptop, I saw the White Rabbit staring at me. This was a surprise! Alice laughed at my reaction and explained, "That is how the White Rabbit felt about the Duchess."

> *The Duchess! The Duchess! Oh my dear paws! Oh my fur and whiskers! She'll get me executed, as sure as ferrets are ferrets!*
> —Alice

What I needed after the abuse was someone who could help me release the pain from my body. Instead, I subconsciously forced the pain deep inside of me. Trauma needs a "mother" figure to calmly accept the rage. I had to wait for sixty years.

9
WHEN SURVIVAL LOOKS LIKE RESILIENCE

In the foreword to my book, *BRAVE*, Dr. Sue wrote, "Janyne McConnaughey may be the most resilient of the resilient clients I saw during many years of therapy" (see Addendum II). To fully understand where this level of resilience began, we will follow small three-year-old Jeannie as she gets up on Sunday, three days after the abuse—the day after sitting on the floor of her bedroom trembling from the trauma. Even after trauma, it was necessary to keep living.

> *In our culture there is a lack of tolerance for the emotional vulnerability [of] traumatized people ... Little time is allotted for the working through of emotional events. We are routinely pressured into adjusting too quickly in the aftermath of an overwhelming situation.*[1]

This chapter is evidence of how children who are reeling from trauma can get up and walk into life with few signs of what happened to them. It doesn't mean the effects aren't brewing inside of them; but it is a rare situation when traumatized children are not expected to move on as if nothing happened.

JEANNIE GETS UP
Alice was watching me type when she suddenly jumped out of her chair, pointed to her black shoes, and proclaimed, "This

---

1. Quoted from: Levine, P. A., *Waking the Tiger: Healing Trauma* (Berkeley, CA: North Atlantic Books, 1997) p.48.

is one of my favorite stories! Jeannie had black shiny shoes just like me! Remember how I tried to explain why they were so shiny?"

'Why, what are your shoes done with?' said the Gry-
phon. 'I mean, what makes them so shiny?' Alice looked
down at them, and considered a little before she gave her
answer. 'They're done with blacking, I believe.'
                       –Alice

"Yes, Alice." I laughed. "This is the story of how Jeannie got dressed in her shiny black shoes. I was so excited to see them again when I re-experienced this memory with EMDR. We do love shiny shoes!"

It was Sunday. Jeannie needed to get up and go to
church as if nothing had happened to her. She felt the
bunk bed move as her brother climbed down; and through
the fog in her head, she tried to figure out where she
was. Then she saw her puppy sitting beside the bed and
remembered.

She needed to go potty but couldn't seem to make herself
move. Fearing what would happen if she didn't get up,
she got her feet out of bed and on the floor and began
to wobble toward the door. Her brother raced past her to
beat her to the bathroom.

"This foot, that foot, this foot, that foot."

This was the singsong dance she did while waiting for
the single bathroom in the small house.

Once in, she said to herself, "I made it! No. No. Don't
look at the bathtub. I don't need a bath!"

Someone was yelling for her to hurry. Her head felt
fuzzy and she just wanted to sit there, but she needed
to let Lee in. As Jeannie came out of the bathroom, her

mother brushed by her and said her clothes were on her bed. Walking to her room, she wondered how she would dress herself. Her dresses were always complicated.

Spotting the dress, shoes and socks, she exclaimed, "Oh! I like this dress! And I get to wear my Sunday shoes! My shiny black shoes!"

She struggled into her dress and pinafore. The skirt got all twisted as she tried to adjust the waistband. Then, when she tried to put on the shoes, she couldn't get the socks right and started crying as she got up and went into the hallway.

"Whoa, Jeannie!" It was Lee. "Need some help?"

He was laughing as he tugged to get her dress in the right place and helped her with her shoes.

"Come on, let's get breakfast." He grabbed her hand and they walked to the kitchen where the Sunday pastry was waiting—but she could only pick at it.

"Jeannie, this is your favorite treat. Are you not hungry?"

"No, I threw up."

He looked concerned and moved back a little. "Well, come on then, we need to go to the car."

She wanted to cry, but she dutifully followed her brother and climbed into the car. Her head still didn't feel right, but she was glad she got her clothes on and made it to the car. Everything she did was very, very hard; but she still needed to go to church.

This memory was of the day my small self learned how to get up and walk again. It wasn't easy, but memories could be "forgotten" and it was important to go to church and not let anyone know what had happened.

Putting all the memories together, I realized this child self could not have understood the medicine the doctor gave my parents to calm her and help her sleep was why her head felt so fuzzy. She was walking in a fog.

This was a Sunday like any other Sunday. My family needed to keep moving as if nothing happened. The cultural and religious ramifications of what happened to me could have destroyed us all.

Jeannie's Imaginary Friend

Dramatic change in a child's behavior is a primary indication that trauma has occurred. My behavior did change, but my outbursts only made my mother angry. This was something I needed to avoid. How I learned to control my trauma behaviors eluded me until I stumbled on the answer during the second year of therapy.

I was helping a friend who was organizing a human trafficking awareness day at the state capitol building in Denver. My assigned task was to go across town to pick up balloons for a display. Upon my return, balloons in tow, I sensed the delight of a child self inside of me as the adult "me" traipsed across the capitol lawn with a huge cluster of inflated balloons.

Leaving the balloons at the designated location, I stopped to view the displays. One display included a small pair of shoes that belonged to a child who was trafficked. Every part of me became absorbed in the horror of this. Then out of the corner of my eye I noticed a video camera.

"Do you mind if I interview you?" a reporter asked. He looked nice enough, but it felt as though he had stolen a piece of me by videoing without permission. I wondered if my unguarded moment looked like trauma. Declining in an oddly wide-eyed way, I joined a passing tour group. While listening to the tour guide, it felt as if there was someone with me besides the child self who loved the balloons. It wasn't a child; instead my child self was talking to some indefinable presence.

As the afternoon passed, the two continued to talk until I exclaimed (very loudly), "You are my imaginary friend!"

Yes, there were a few odd looks.

So much made sense! The Watcher who appeared on the scene during the Three Chair's integration, was a gatekeeper—a common component of dissociative systems. He kept Jeannie's memory behind the gate, but was also the grand controller of the system. As the Three Chairs integrated, his role diminished and by the time my child selves surfaced, he was in distress. He guarded my stories for a lifetime and now I was sitting on a couch telling the secrets. Everything was completely out of control.

I could feel both the distress and the strong protective stance of the presence hovering over the child self who surfaced while I was carrying the balloons. This presence, which I came to know as The Watcher, was an evolved form of my imaginary friend.

The roles The Watcher fulfilled in the system were much like the executive functions a preschool child should have been developing. Instead of developing these skills, my child self's clever subconscious created an imaginary friend to help her behave. Her ever-present puppy was a logical choice.

This epiphany explained how Jeannie controlled the chaos and protected herself from her mother's anger. This imaginary friend who became The Watcher explained my extraordinary ability to control trauma-related behaviors throughout my life. I also now understood why I kept the stuffed puppy for sixty years and got it out of the box when the memory of the abuse began surfacing.

When Children Go Silent

Though the abuse occurred when I was three, the effects lived on in Four. She was a quiet child self and unlikely to ask for help. As discussed in the previous chapter, Three expressed her trauma outwardly; Four withdrew into silence and deadness.

It was hard to find Four and even harder to help her. This four-year-old child self felt like a gap in my memories. No one would have recognized her silence as depression. The pain in Four was easy to miss. My behavior was probably much easier to manage.

Four was so quiet, I convinced myself she appeared to move on with her life as if nothing happened. Logically, this didn't seem remotely possible.

As she surfaced, I felt myself distance from her. I didn't want to feel the deadness inside of her, because adult me also felt dead inside. I thought this might just be how healing felt. It certainly wasn't what I hoped for, but it was possible this might be how I would feel for the rest of my life and I needed to adjust. Life had to go on. Resignation was my only coping skill.

Jeannie Sits on Her Hands

Dr. Sue and I met to go over edits for *BRAVE*. She noted that I was not fully expressing the turbulent feelings I experienced in therapy. I was trying to be objective about what she was telling me. Then, I sat on my hands.

I knew it was Four. She still needed help and, right in the middle of working on the book, she sat on her hands. My sudden shift from an adult to a child self, who was now swinging her feet and looking intently at Dr. Sue, was obvious to both of us.

Struggling to ground myself in an adult form, I asked, "Should we make an appointment?"

Dr. Sue reached for her appointment book.

Back on the couch, I tried to not be frustrated with this child self who was still hurting. The memory that surfaced was filled with nightmares. My dad came and sat beside me and tried to calm me so I would go back to sleep.

"It's only a dream, Jeannie. You are OK, you can go back to sleep," he would say.

But it wasn't a dream. I was reliving the trauma. He had been told I would forget. He was trying to help me by telling me it was a dream. When I would wake and not find him there, I would scream in terror, and he would rush in to comfort me so I wouldn't wake my brothers and Mother. The bond between us grew as we were surviving together.

It took two sessions and days of processing to fully understand how dark those days were for my small self. I hadn't moved on unscathed. Not even close.

While processing with EMDR, I felt myself wander around the house and felt the deadness inside me. I didn't want to eat. I didn't want to play. I didn't want to do anything.

For weeks, I felt dead and there were times when I was frantic and felt like I could barely stay in my own skin. Without a busy life to distract me, the full effects of how Jeannie felt each day became evident, and the deadness was intense.

While trying to process, I researched "early childhood depression." What I found documented what I sensed—depression in very young children is possible and alters brain development.[2] My lifelong battle with depression began as a young child.

Like my parents, I failed to understand the depth of care

---

2. For more information: Dryden, J., "Early Childhood Depression Alters Brain Development," (December 16, 2015). Retrieved from: https://source.wustl.edu/2015/12/early-childhood-depression-alters-brain-development

required to heal a small, traumatized child. I kept thinking my child self was fine and walking away—only to have her surface again with another layer of pain. She sat on her hands to tell us she still needed help. I learned to never ignore the quiet child.

PROTECTING JEANNIE AND HOW SHE THREW UP AGAIN

My parents did try to protect me after that terrible day. About a month before my dad died, we were talking. I asked him if I had gone with him when he went to work at the campground.

He said, "Well, yes, you must have always gone with me, because we never left you anywhere."

This was true. My dad took me to the church or campground with him, or my mother took me to school with her. She taught kindergarten at the Sandia Base elementary school in a white, barrack-type building with wooden floors. She obtained permission to keep me with her, since I was too young to attend. I could do the work with the other students, but it was important not to bother her.

One day, I needed to throw up, but I didn't dare leave the room. I walked up and stood in front of her desk and stared at her. I couldn't talk.

"Jeannie, you know you are not allowed to bother me. Why are you standing there?"

At first, I was afraid to talk, but then it became impossible because the nauseous waves were in my throat. The wave exploded on her desk and across the floor. The children in the room recoiled in noisy disgust. We all smelled the awfulness.

Sent to the bathroom in humiliation, I cried until I was sure no more was coming up. Carefully peeking out the bathroom door, I saw the janitor walking toward me.

"Jeannie, are you OK? You made a big mess in there for me." He was smiling.

"I was trying to tell her I needed to throw up."

He tousled my hair and sent me back to the classroom.

Ᏸ

Jeannie, who was watching me type, sighed loudly.

"She should have listened to me. She should have seen I was sick. She should not have raised her eyebrow at me. I would have told her what was wrong. I stayed on a mat until Daddy came for me. I was shivering. He came and took me home."

"Yes, Jeannie. You are right. You were trying to tell her!"

Without warning, I burst into laughter.

Jeannie looked at me in surprise and then she started laughing too. "Ewww! It was awful! It smelled terrible. It got all over her desk and some of the papers!"

Ᏸ

When I mentioned this incident to my dad, he told me, "Yes, when you threw up, we had to get your brother out of the room or he would throw up too." It appears my vomiting was a familiar family problem. It is completely possible this incident was the flu, but certainly some of my frequent vomiting was due to trauma.

The next memory of vomiting was the day Five went to the party. I don't remember vomiting again after that—not until around fifty five when I became ill with a badly diseased gall bladder. We knew it was serious because, until then, Scott had never known me to throw up in over twenty-five years of marriage—not even through months of pregnancy and morning sickness. I tried desperately to get rid of the wretchedness in my stomach, but there was no gag reflex.

But while in therapy, I would wake in the night and dash (well, in an RV, it is more like climb) to the bathroom. Convinced it was the flu, it surprised me to wake up fine in the morning. I was trying to release trauma exactly as I had when I was small.

CONTROLLING MYSELF

Jeannie was watching me type. I felt how strong she was. Time and time again in therapy, she clamped down with all her strength to control some behavior. She made herself stop crying. She forced herself to not act out her anger. She subconsciously "forgot" the bad memories. She stopped herself from feeling most body sensations and apparently rid herself of her own gag reflex. Her strength amazed me.

Many behavioral signs indicated I was struggling, but my ability to get up and walk masked most of them. Yes, there were bad dreams; yes, I threw up; but I wasn't screaming at my mother anymore. I was so quiet; surely this meant I was OK.

I was surviving, and it looked like resilience.

Alice, whose armchair was starting to show signs of all the dragging back and forth, said, "Never be fooled by the apparent resilience of a child."

Jeannie looked serious as she reflected, "That was like you in Wonderland. Your adventures got really confusing and hard sometimes, but you appeared to be taking it all in stride. I did that too."

"True," said Alice. "But I was horribly confused sometimes. Especially by the Dormouse!"

Everyone nodded in agreement. Alice's conversation with the dormouse during the tea party really was confusing.

I looked down to see my four-year-old self nodding off (much like the dormouse was so apt to do). She was sucking on her middle two fingers. I leaned over, kissed her on the forehead and picked her up to carry her to bed. I remembered how comforted she was when Daddy carried her to bed.

She mumbled with contentment as I tucked her in. It was the end of a busy day! I tucked her white puppy in beside her and left the small night-light on. I was a bit hesitant to leave her; but as I turned to walk out the door, I found Alice dragging her armchair into the room. She curled up in the chair next to Jeannie and I retrieved another blanket to cover her.

As I began to close the door, I heard Alice reading about the King meeting the Cheshire Cat.

> *'It's a friend of mine—a Cheshire Cat,' said Alice.*
> *'Allow me to introduce it.'*
> —Alice

Jeannie looked up at Alice and said, "The Cheshire Cat was your friend. Just like you and my puppy are *my* friends."

I smiled as the door clicked shut. Often my fantasies were the only places I felt safe. Alice had become another imaginary friend for my small self, Jeannie, whose creative mind had helped her survive. It looked very much like resilience.

10
THE LiFE EVERY CHiLD DESERVES[1]

Before I began therapy, I went through a period where I became increasingly irritated by people saying they deserved things. While working on this book, I found a random document I created during that time. It only included the following definition and the lyrics to a song about getting what you deserve.

Deserve: To be entitled to, as a result of past actions; to be worthy to have.

Outwardly, I felt I deserved to live a good life; but underneath, I felt much like the gardeners Alice met in the Queen's garden.

'I heard the Queen say only yesterday you deserved to be beheaded!'
            –Alice

Alice, who was sitting across the kitchen table from me, spoke. "The Queen was frightening! She thought almost everyone deserved to be beheaded."

I shuddered. "Yes, she really was awful."

I am thankful something in me decided to not believe

1. Borelli, J. L., "Separation Is Never Ending: Attachment Is a Human Right," (June 23, 2018). Retrieved from https://www.psychologytoday.com/us/blog/thriving/201806/separation-is-never-ending-attachment-is-human-right

the "queen" of self-loathing and instead tried to live the life I deserved. What every child deserves is a primary caregiver completely (wholeheartedly) devoted to meeting relational needs. It is this deeply-secure relationship that gives a child the security to begin to explore the world.

This chapter focuses on the first One Who Lives, the Explorer, and her twin, The One Who Cries. This initial dissociative split enabled me to live my life and explore with courageous abandon. To do this, it was necessary to leave the trauma and attachment wounds in the bed with her sister.

What follows is processing I did during therapy with the help of The Storyteller. These are transcriptions of the original EMDR processing of memories that surfaced early in the second year of therapy. In these situations I may sound like a detached stranger, but there are indications that I was beginning to develop a relationship with my child selves.

THE SMALL EXPLORER

I had finished my morning coffee and was sitting at the kitchen table. I planned to spend the morning writing, but just as I finished the introduction, Six, the One Who Lives, called out to me. "I'm headed to the creek, would you like to come along?"

I got up to follow her.

She said, "I thought you might like to go to the creek with me. My family has a cabin at the campgrounds, and it's my favorite place to go in the summer. My mother doesn't like it there, but the rest of us do. When Daddy takes me there, he works to help build things. But he lets me run and play all day long. There is only one place I am not supposed to go—the creek; but I am going there today. No one will know."

It seemed I should probably be the adult and caution her. I asked, "You aren't supposed to go there?"

"Well, no. But my mother is just afraid of water. There is no reason to be afraid of water! I know how to be careful! How silly to think I will fall in the creek; it isn't even deep. There are also mountain lions, but they won't be there this time of day."

These really did sound like valid reasons to forbid the creek, but I followed along behind her as she skipped down the path. She seemed careful when she got to the creek, so I settled on a log to watch her. She gathered sticks and, one by one, she threw them into the water, then ran chasing them down the stream. Then she gathered small rocks and hid them under a larger rock. She certainly was enjoying herself!

"Jeannie, Jeannie, where are you?" a voice called.

I saw her flinch and run toward the trees to hide.

"Jeannie, we need you to come right now!"

A loud whistle echoed across the creek. It was my dad's distinctive whistle. I watched as Jeannie shrank into the rocks and bushes. I could see the fear on her face. Slowly the voices faded into the distance.

"Who was that?" I asked. Even though I recognized the whistle and voice as belonging to my dad, I wanted to hear her answer.

"My daddy and my brother. I didn't want them to find me here. I would be in big trouble."

She continued to watch the path closely and mumbled, "If I go back to the playground they will find me there."

LEFT BEHIND

She was off! As I moved more slowly, it took a few minutes to catch up with her at the playground where, by now, she was swinging. She motioned for me to stay back as she swung. We stayed there a long time.

It began to get darker as the sun set behind the trees. Voices could be heard singing in the tabernacle near the playground. I walked toward the swinging child but could not get her attention. Her eyes stared back without seeing me as she got off the swing and began to walk down the gravel road toward a row of cabins.

I followed her in the fading light and watched her climb up steps into a cabin. Hearing her cry, I climbed up after her.

"Is this your cabin?" I asked.

Through her sobs she answered, "Yes, but they aren't here. They didn't come and find me at the playground. I was bad, very bad, and now they have left me. When they called, I hid just like Adam and Eve, and now they have left me here because I am so bad. The light is too high for me to reach. I am afraid of the dark, and there isn't a flashlight to go find someone."

It was doubtful they left her, but it did seem odd. And she needed me to help her out of the predicament in which she had found herself.

"What if you walk to where the lights are and I follow along behind you? Will that help?"

The sobbing slowed. "Yes, it will help. I am very brave, you know. I went to the creek by myself. I can go find help. Someone will take care of me."

Going for Help

Climbing back down the stairs, she was off. Yes, she was brave. The path was dark by this time, and at one point she heard rustling in the bushes and began talking to herself.

"It is not a mountain lion. They would stay on the path. Maybe it is a deer. Deer won't hurt me."

Up ahead, the path widened and the snack shack came into view. There were people talking and laughing all around.

"Jeannie! What are you doing here? We thought you must have gone with your parents!"

She looked confused and asked, "Where did they go? I was swinging and no one came and got me for dinner. I'm hungry."

"Oh, my! What would you like?"

"7-Up and peanuts!"

The laughter embraced her and one of the adults walked off to fetch the treat while another began explaining.

"Your brother broke his arm and they took him to town to the doctor. They were searching and calling for you. We thought they found you and took you with them, or we would have kept looking."

By now she was dumping the peanuts in the 7-Up and drinking the rare treat. The adults continued talking about the confusion and how horrible it must have been for this little girl who got left behind. The headlights of a car appeared, and they formed a protective ring around her as the car drove closer.

WHEN MOTHER RETURNED

A petite woman exploded into the circle and began pinching the child's arm with her finely sharpened fingernails as she dragged her away.

"Where were you? We called and called for you. You must have heard us! Were you somewhere you weren't supposed to be? Did you go to the graveyard?"

Abruptly, I became the small child....

She is dragging me from the circle! I was brave; but now everyone thinks I was naughty. I don't want to say I went to the creek. I will lie. I will tell her I went to the graveyard.

Feeling the couch beneath me, I heard a voice pulling me back from the edge of despair.

I could feel the hot flush of shame as I opened my eyes. "The kind adults who bought the 7-Up and peanuts looked so sad. I thought I saw the shame of my naughtiness on their faces, but they were probably just sad for me because I was so brave and then was humiliated."

Shame was rolling off me in waves. As we talked, Dr. Sue confirmed my need to not be humiliated and to have a parent who would take me to the creek to play. I also needed to feel safe enough not to lie and needed my mother to tell me I was brave!

My adult mind was trying to make sense of this memory. Over the years, this had never been the way I had told what happened that day. I tried to make the memory fit my version of the story, but during EMDR my mind would only tell the truth.

I always said I was swinging and it got dark, so I walked to the snack shop to find help. There was much truth in this story, but also much lost. The little girl on the swing, fearing she was left, dissociated and remembered nothing of her dark journey to the cabin. Going to the creek and hiding was also repressed. As my mind searched to understand, I drifted back into the memory with the small child.

Forgetting the Pain

Mommy is shoving me into the front seat, and the car is bouncing up the rocky road to our cabin. I am confused, and she is angry. I am crawling into bed and crying. I want someone to hold me and say how brave I am. I hear her heels clip clopping around the cabin. She is so angry!

When this memory surfaced, I didn't yet know my mother

shook me and didn't recognize it, but now as I look back at my EMDR processing of the memory, I see it clearly. I felt my small body begin to clamp down on the memory. The intensity and force of "shoving" the memory deep into my mind was tremendous. I stopped crying and sank into a trance.

My adult self knew this process. It was how I learned to forget memories. I would walk down a path again and again toward a "do not enter" sign until the memory didn't surface. This skill was developed to an art form.

Hearing small footsteps, I looked up. Both Sixes stood in front of me. The One Who Lives handed the memory to the One Who Cries, and she crawled into bed and began crying again.

I asked, "Is this why you cry?"

"It's one reason," she said between sobs. "There are many others, but mostly I try not to remember, or maybe I don't remember."

Looking down at the small child in the bed, I whispered, "I am sorry this happened to you."

Looking At Her Watch

While the experience of going to the creek and the events in the cabin were traumatic, most interactions with my mother were common daily happenings.

The Storyteller looked up at me and said, "The two Sixes had terrible problems with our mother. Sometimes she was mean, but other times she just ignored us. She looked at her watch but not at us."

I understood this immediately. "You are thinking about my reaction when Dr. Sue looked at her watch, aren't you? Do you want to write that story?"

She smiled. "You tell it and I will type."

And so, I began....

☙

It was at the end of a therapy session, and Dr. Sue looked at her watch. As my dissociation made it difficult to get me in a good place to leave, her care and patience seemed unending; but she really did need to check the time by looking at her watch or one of the clocks in the room. Many other times when this had happened, I had completely dysregulated. This time I laughed and said, "It is OK if you look at your watch."

She smiled at me and asked if I was sure.

Yes, I was sure. But feeling comfortable had only come after I had processed a seemingly random memory. This is the memory that helped me understand my hypervigilance.

> *I have a book in my hands, the story of The Three Bears. I know all the words and I can read! I am carrying the book to my mother. "Listen to me! I can read this!"*
>
> *I began "reading" the words I had tried to memorize. I heard my mother correct me and saw her look at her watch, one she wore for years. She was twisting the black-cord wristband to look at the time. Then she stood up and walked away.*

I opened my eyes and exclaimed, "She would dismiss me by looking at her watch! When I didn't catch the hint, she got up and walked away. When you look at your watch, I think you are saying we are done and I am being dismissed!"

It was a trigger which took some time to resolve; so on this day, when I told Dr. Sue she could look at her watch, it was a big accomplishment.

With the memory and trigger fully processed, we laughed about how I always noticed when she looked at her watch— even when she thought I was looking the other way!

There were many work-related situations when I had

become instantly consumed by what I now understand was shame, but I could never have told you that it was because someone looked at a watch.

This watch trigger demonstrates how the lower brain, wired for survival, can see danger and react before the "thinking" brain ever comes online. Children wired for hypervigilance are constantly monitoring facial or environmental cues, and when triggered, they react immediately with a fight, flight, or freeze response. It is a survival instinct. Hypervigilance robbed me of much of the joy in life that I truly deserved.

When triggered, the thinking brain doesn't engage. Children cannot reflect on the situation, because it is an instinctual reaction. Asking them, "What were you thinking?" is a completely ineffective question. They weren't.

When triggered as a child, asking me to explain what happened and come up with a better choice would have resulted in some great creative storytelling that might have looked like I was lying. I would have written down whatever I believed the teacher wanted me to say.

WITHOUT RELATIONSHIP

Even without trauma, situations like my "reading" memory are common. Mothers are busy. They have things to do. I would never suggest it is always possible to listen to children the length of time they would like, but when relationship exists, it is feasible to end the conversation with relational care.

Recent Facebook posts about entitled and demanding children have received a following, but they miss the root causes of needs-based behavior. The assumption seems to be that the entitlement is because parents give in to them and make sure they get everything for which they ask. I doubt this is the true problem.

My mother was not present as I was "reading." I was a

determined child and would eventually demand to be heard. It may have seemed that I got everything I wanted, but the truth was I got everything I demanded. I was trying to have my needs met—to receive what I knew I deserved. I didn't learn this skill by being given everything I asked for. I learned it by fighting for what I needed or felt I deserved. This may look the same from the outside, but the inner motivations and needs are very different.

Many children (and adults) who are accustomed to fighting for everything, appear demanding and combative. I remembered times when this was true in my life, but never understood why I felt it necessary to fight for things I merely could have requested. My inner assumption was that no one was really interested in what I needed. As I grew older I became better at getting my needs met in more subtle ways, which likely was perceived as manipulation.

In our busy world, it is hard to always be present for our children. Sometimes the solution is to give them what they ask for instead of giving them our exhausted selves. I was often there as a mother. Every caregiver has been there. The difference in my personal childhood story was the lack of relationship with my mother. I couldn't say to myself, "She is busy, but she loves me." This is what all children need to believe—what every child deserves.[2]

Working As a Team

The Storyteller and I worked at the kitchen table for some time. The two Sixes took turns sitting across from us to fill in the details.

---

2. The book, *Llama, Llama, Red Pajama*, by Anna Dewdney is a perfect illustration of a busy mother, the distress of a child who needs attention, and the importance of repair in relationships.

I reflected, "It seems like we should have placed the Mother Doll in *this* chapter. What do you think?"

The One Who Lives looked at her sister who was also thinking about this.

She said, "No one knew about me the first time we saw the Mother Doll. I was hiding, but the eyebrow—"

"That's right!" I responded. "This chapter is about how I got to know both of you and how you helped me live the life I deserved. Nothing yet made sense to me when you first had a melt down over the Mother Doll."

Alice was pulling her armchair into the kitchen while listening intently. Things not making sense made sense to her. She laughed and said, "When you shifted, you felt like I did when I was talking to the caterpillar!"

'I can't explain myself, I'm afraid, sir,' said Alice,
'because I'm not myself, you see.'

Alice was right. "No, I really didn't feel like myself, and it didn't make sense," I said. "But now I know I really was myself and I did make sense."

In one voice, the Sixes exclaimed, "We did make sense! We just wanted to go exploring at the creek and have a mother who cared about us. Maybe even a mother who would take us to the creek. She didn't do that, but you did!"

"Yes," I said. "I did what you needed. We enjoyed our adventures at the creek, didn't we?"

The Sixes smiled. They both went to the creek with me, unlike when the One Who Lives went to the creek and left her twin crying in the bed.

Relational care is what every child deserves. It is the foundation that helps them explore the world. These twins finally experienced what they deserved—first with Dr. Sue and then with me as I became enough for myself. Taking my child selves to the creek, throwing sticks, and collecting rocks looked like playing, which was important for me to experience; but it was also the process of building the relationship my child selves deserved.

⁊

Everyone sat back in their chairs with a look of satisfaction. I was just getting ready to close my laptop, when the seven-year-old twins walked into the kitchen.

"Are you ready to begin your chapter?" I asked.

"Yes, we are," they answered. "Our hammer and boxes are ready, and we are excited!"

I smiled at their excitement, which was no longer mixed with trauma.

11
A TANGLE OF FEELINGS AND EMOTIONS

While the Sixes were the first to wrestle with the feelings elicited by the Mother Doll, they would not be the last. Some time later, when the Mother Doll was placed in the chair again, the reaction was still explosive. This was our introduction to who I would come to know as Seven and later understand as the Girl with the Hammer and the Keeper of the Cave of Memories.

The journey of the Sevens was one of separating and processing feelings and emotions. This was no small task for a child who subconsciously connected them all to trauma.

Now the Sevens settled themselves on the kitchen chairs to help fill in the details for their chapter. They looked eager to begin and much less anxious than when they first surfaced.

Alice was so calm, she appeared to have fallen asleep in her armchair. Everyone decided she should just take a nap.

Much of this chapter describes the subconscious workings of dissociation.[1] While dissociation, a natural coping mechanism, protected me from consciously remembering traumatic memories, it also interfered with the normal process of storing memories in the brain.

The trauma froze parts of me at various developmental stages

---

1. Living in dissociative parts feels very different from life as a "whole" self. Seven can be a single child self, one part of twin selves, or two child selves with one voice. Embrace the dissociative dissonance!

with the memories, feelings, emotions, and internalized messages. Each part took on roles that met developmental and emotional needs so I could function. This is much the same as children maturing and integrating new roles as part of their "self," but my "roles" never integrated, lived as separate child selves, and surfaced as complete personalities.

Even though it seemed like it would be too much to absorb, the Sevens appeared to appreciate the explanation of how they came to be. In one voice, they said, "You didn't make us up. We were real. We were doing our best to help you live."

"Yes! You were real and you certainly did help me. I knew you were different from Six by how you reacted to the Mother Doll. Maybe we should start there."

The two nodded their heads in agreement.

Hearing the Mother Doll mentioned again, Alice woke up and dragged her armchair close to the table to listen to the story.

THE MOTHER DOLL RETURNS

I watched Dr. Sue get up from the chair and walk over to pick up the Mother Doll. Weeks had passed since I became hysterical over the eyebrow. Was the memory resolved? I wasn't sure, but as soon as she picked up the doll, I cried, "No!" and collapsed into fearful tears.

At first, we thought it was still Six, but it didn't feel like her. This was a different child self. When asked how old I felt, I realized I felt seven. We understood Seven—the Keeper of the Cave of Memories boxed up the bad things that happened—but this appeared to be her twin who lived.

I immediately felt anxious. This Seven held crushing anxiety. I was suddenly unable to distinguish between any of my emotions or feelings. They were all tangled and everything felt like trauma and fear.

This session occurred right before Scott and I were to leave on a trip. The Seven who lived surfaced with such force that I struggled to stay grounded as we left town.

SEVEN GOES ON A TRIP

Scott's work-related trip took us to San Diego—one of my favorite places. We didn't expect to take my seven-year-old self with us, but since it was completely unpredictable when she might surface, it seemed logical to accept her presence and enjoy the trip as a family.

It appeared that any experience out of the daily routine was a trigger that caused Seven to surface. Going on a trip certainly fit the bill. I felt her anxiety as we drove to the airport. Turning a corner in the terminal, we came almost face to face with one of the biggest planes we had ever seen. I sat transfixed as Scott went to buy lunch.

On our way to the terminal, I nearly fell trying to get on the people mover. As I sat looking at the plane, I thought about how my feet didn't seem to be doing anything in my normal manner. I stood up and tried to take a step with my dominant right foot, but the foot refused. I was now left-footed.

We ate our lunch and headed toward the gate. Approaching the escalator, I wasn't sure how I would navigate with my left foot leading the way. Before I could step onto the escalator, several men who looked like a group of old college friends enjoying a trip together arrived from the other direction. To my dismay, they motioned for me to go first.

They looked at me oddly as I implored, "Please go ahead of me. It is a long story, but just go ahead of me."

Laughing, they continued down the escalator and I cautiously tried to step on with my right foot—but involuntarily switched to my left. Scott watched this little dance and then steadied me as we continued down the escalator.

I thought back to when I was seven years old. I remembered wearing corrective shoes. I wondered if wearing the shoes related to this. It was a fascinating insight as to how dissociative parts not only have specific personality traits, but can also have different physical attributes.

The Day at the Beach

I was excited to take Seven to San Diego. I wanted her to experience the ocean. It seemed she never lived the experiences of the older child selves. For one child self to not know the experience of another was common. It was interesting to note what she had experienced.

"Hula Hoops!" she exclaimed with delight when someone went down the beach twirling one. Then, she stood transfixed by a hummingbird whose breast glowed red in the sunlight. My adult body ran from waves and squealed when a wave overtook her and soaked her pant legs.

As we ate lunch, a family came down the boardwalk with a red wagon full of Girl Scout cookies. The Girl Scout's brother was wearing a "sandwich sign" with prices.

Seven exclaimed, "They are helping her sell the cookies! My family never helped me! Today is Sunday. I couldn't sell them on Sunday!"

Seven was happy to see the girl's family helping her. I remembered how my mother bribed me to drop out of Brownies because of the hassles surrounding cookie sales. I felt happy right along with Seven.

It was a wonderful day at the beach, and later in the afternoon we decided to drive to La Jolla. As soon as we got near the cliffs, I felt Seven begin to panic. This was my first inkling of where my fear of mountain roads and cliffs began. We stopped to sit on a bench and Scott walked over toward the edge.

I heard myself scream, *"Stop, don't go near the edge! Come back!"*

Scott was not appreciative of my yelling at him like an errant child. I couldn't blame him, but Seven was clearly in distress as I sat on the bench sobbing.

GOING TO SANDIA PEAK

After enjoying San Diego for several days, I returned home and headed back to therapy. By this time, I was sure what happened at the La Jolla cliffs somehow connected to a family trip to Sandia Peak.

Seven would have longed to go to the top of Sandia Peak, a mountain that had looked down on her since the day she was born. I had a memory of crawling to the edge and looking over the city. That was it. But I knew I had gone there. I wondered what happened at the top of the mountain? Online I found pictures of the overlook. I could see why the steepness of the cliffs in La Jolla triggered Seven's memory. Seven was ready to tell the story of Sandia Peak.

> *The car is stopping. My brother and I jump out and run for the stairs. I want to be first! He is pushing me! My mother is screaming. "Stop! Don't go too near the edge!" I am at the top. There is a fence. She is still screaming. I am crawling to look over at the city.*

My memory was correct. I looked up the history of Sandia Peak and found out the road was paved to the top about the time I was Seven. We would have wanted to drive on it. I imagine the entire city wanted to drive on the newly-paved road.

I can also understand my mother, who was afraid of mountain roads, probably didn't enjoy the drive. And then seeing two of her children jostling to the edge of a cliff would have terrified her. Her screaming combined with the view at the top of the stairs convinced my anxious seven-year-old self I truly was in danger.

Had I screamed at Scott the same way my mother screamed at me? It seemed plausible. The voices sounded the same.

This trip took place before the memory surfaced of the cliff where I almost ended my life at twenty three. It was certainly a foreshadowing of things to come; but for the moment, my processing explained why fear and excitement mixed in a way the Sevens were not able to separate. I knew this tangle of feelings and emotions well because my abuse occurred after playing blocks with the man in the day care. Happiness and fear were always tangled.

Seven and the Journal of Feelings

Every difficult emotion felt the same to Seven. Fearful? Sad? Angry? They all held trauma. Every single one of them.

Knowing we wouldn't be able to do much unless this child self began to distinguish between emotions, I found a blank journal, chose an emotion, wrote it on a page, looked up the definition, then drew pictures to illustrate the meaning. Pure emotions were easier to define than feelings, which were often almost indefinable and usually resulted in a picture of a memory. This was "Seven's journal." Later, while working on this chapter, I found the journal and was both delighted and saddened by the pictures inside. The drawings were a depiction of my dual life. Some pages were about Scott's and my San Diego adventure, but other pages depicted deep processing of emotional trauma.

One drawing portrayed a boarded-up path between two trees. I was beginning to glimpse the Seven who held the hammer and distinguish her from the one I previously found in the Cave of Memories. At the beginning of the journal, Seven was a single child. She was boarding up a path between the trees, but I had no idea the Cave of Memories was behind the boards.

Finally, on a page midway through the journal, I saw both twins. I wrote, "Of course there are two!"

The power of the subconscious mind to hide the obvious is truly astounding.

Putting Up and Taking Down Boards

Understanding the Sevens and their role in containing, keeping, and protecting me from memories was a fascinating journey. In hindsight, the Girl with the Hammer began building shelves to help her sister store the boxed-up memories. Only much later would the memories start oozing out of the cave and young adult Jane tell her to board up the entrance. This Seven twin was busy fulfilling the "boarding-up" role when she surfaced.

Dreams often revealed my subconscious thoughts. Some dreams were mentioned in *BRAVE*, but this one was buried in my processing files. The following is a portion of an email between sessions.

> *I have had life-long, recurring dreams/thoughts about a path. I am walking on it when I see the path is blocked and boarded up. There are layers of boards and hundreds of nails to keep them secure. I know I shouldn't remove them. I always quickly turn back.*

The terror of taking down the first board during EMDR was overpowering. Concealed behind the boards was the emotional pain and confusion incurred by never talking about or processing the trauma. It didn't feel safe to pull them down by myself.

Embracing Emotions and Feelings

It was important to understand feelings were not negative or positive—they were simply informative bodily sensations. All emotions and feelings had a purpose. I also needed to separate the trauma from normal feelings and emotions. I didn't need to fear being happy.

Seven and I both needed to develop ways to calm my debilitating anxiety. She helped me do this in one beneficial way. At her age, my parents owned a record player and a big "binder" of classical music records. She may have been the only one to play them and was sad when we moved and left them behind. When I remembered this, I introduced her to an instrumental station on Pandora. The music, along with her drawing and coloring, helped me begin to calm my ever-present anxiety in healthy ways.

Finally, at sixty two, Seven learned what she had needed to know as a child. Held tightly in boxes, and behind boards, all trauma-filled feelings would eventually surface in frightening ways. Released, they flowed over her in waves—some pounding like a raging sea, but repeated processing allowed them to fade.

Effective processing of trauma-related emotional material is essential. This requires more than merely talking about trauma (which can sometimes re-traumatize). But thinking the trauma will fade if not talked about is never the answer.

In addition, running from all feelings meant I couldn't embrace joy. There were many experiences, especially those surrounding significant days, that got tangled up with the pain and needed reframing.

Of Mother's Day and Choosing Cards

The second episode with the Mother Doll was evidence that both Six and Seven struggled with the relationship with my mother. Of the many roles a mother fulfills, helping her children understand and embrace emotions may be the one mentioned least often. To our detriment, many Western traditions belittle the role of feelings and emotions in our lives. The result is the diminishment, disregard, avoidance, and mistrust of a crucial part of being human.

The two frozen child selves my subconscious utilized to deal with all my feelings and emotions lived a life of sacrifice to enable me to live. Yet, their inability to understand, feel, heal, or embrace any of the feelings held in boxes, robbed me of much that could have filled my life with joy.

Despite working through layers of mother issues, the approaching day in honor of mothers was still bringing dread. I made much progress in accepting my mother's role in my story and the probable trauma in hers; but I still dreaded Mother's Day. Years of standing in the card isle trying to find a card that said nothing, haunted me—even after her death. My inherent determination to be honest to myself (which I found in Five), made it an all but impossible situation. The card needed to speak the truth.

The Sevens and I were discussing the problem when the two eight-year-old child selves arrived in the kitchen to help us. I needed to be sure every part of me knew their mother was no longer alive.

"You know we don't have to get cards anymore, right?"

I saw two of my child selves roll their eyes at me. It wasn't a great start, but it was a beginning. Of course they knew their mother had died several years earlier—but there was still some confusion about this.

The Sevens, who were finally beginning to feel emotions, said, "Yes, but the cards are lovely and say wonderful things about mothers. I just wish we could have chosen one of them."

The eight-year-old Problem Solver jumped in. "Yes, that's it! We understand we didn't have a mother who loved us like those who buy those cards. We accept this. But there were others who cared about us. It isn't like we haven't ever felt loved."

They all nodded in agreement. There were many who fit this description, but I knew there was only one person on their mind. The Problem Solver's sister voiced the name they all were thinking.

"Dr. Sue. She is the one who helped us know what a mother who loved us would have felt like. I mean, she wasn't our mother; but she cared about us in ways our mother should have."

The Girl with the Hammer, who was always the one to take action, jumped up to propose a plan. "If we tell her we know she isn't our mother, could we go pick out a Mother's Day card? You know, one that tells what she did for us. Do you think it would be OK?"

It was brilliant! My child selves were learning to reframe their own stories. I smiled at them and said, "I will call her and explain what we need to do to reframe how we feel about Mother's Day. She will understand."

I was right. She did understand. We weren't looking for a mother, we merely wanted to describe all the ways she showed us how it felt to be cared about like our mother should have. We needed to stand in the card isle and feel all the emotions meant to be felt and expressed on Mother's Day.

I went to Target and stood in the card isle. It felt much like being in a candy store. There were so many options! So many wonderful things I could say! I looked at every card until I found one that said she helped me learn to fly. This was true in many ways, but especially as a writer. Yes, this is exactly what a mother or a good therapist can do—convince us we can fly and provide a safe space to grow and/or heal until it is possible.

Handing the card to Dr. Sue was the final piece the Sevens needed for healing. When Scott joined the effort by giving flowers along with the card, everyone smiled. Emotions were pure and good and *felt* all around.

"Oh, that was beautiful!" It was Alice. We were completely unaware of her sitting in her armchair watching the entire exchange of card and flowers.

Alice explained, "It is somewhat like my sister said at the end of my book. Something about how you will now feel sorrow—but find pleasure in simple joys—while remembering this newly-framed child life."

Alice wiped the tears from her eyes and began to drag her armchair to the next chapter. It was time to hand the story over to the Eights.

"You're up next," the Sevens said in one voice to the two Eights, who had helped solve the Mother's Day problem.

12
OF LiES AND FORGETTiNG

*I can't remember things as I used—and I don't keep the
same size for ten minutes together!*

–Alice

I didn't believe I experienced the amnesia that plagues most
with Dissociative Identity Disorder (DID), but there was no
doubt I met all the other criteria. While I was in therapy,
the American Psychiatric Association (APA) was in the process
of revising the diagnostic manual. Before the revision, an allowance was made for classifying dissociative disorders without gaps
in the recall of everyday events (DID NOS—"DID Not Otherwise Specified"). In the revised DSM 5,[1] the NOS designation
was removed along with this allowance. While I understand this
change in the designation (mainly for insurance/diagnostic reasons), I do not agree with removing the allowance for no loss of
memory. I also believe clients would be better served by viewing
dissociation as a spectrum disorder.

Viewing DID as a survival coping mechanism makes sense
and helps me understand that I subconsciously built additional
coping strategies to prevent what occurred in the following
memory. Until helping the Eights, I didn't understand memory
lapses *were* a problem as a child.

It was common, while processing with EMDR, to experience
more than one part of my dissociative system. The first time this

---

1. American Psychiatric Association, *Diagnostic and Statistical Manual of
Mental Disorders, 5th* (Arlington, VA: Author, 2013).

happened was when I "saw" the twin six-year-old child selves. Then, by the time the eight-year-old memory told in this chapter surfaced, I understood exactly what had happened.

The Eights were now sitting at the kitchen table, ready to tell their story. Alice settled into the armchair she had dragged from the previous chapter. The Storyteller's fingers hovered over the keyboard. She had been waiting since Part I to write about this Easter memory. It explained so much!

The Easter Basket and the Chocolate Bunny

Eight-year-old Jeannie sat on the bed staring at the cellophane-wrapped Easter basket. She begged to have an Easter basket like the other children who came to church on Easter, but it was never part of our family traditions. By a stroke of luck, it seems that someone gave my mother a basket, that they had won, as a gift.

Jeannie's mother deposited the basket in the bedroom with a grunt of "Here. Now you can stop begging."

Jeannie wasn't allowed to eat any candy until after church, and then she would have to share it with her brother. She was still sitting on the bed when she "saw" the child, who looked exactly like her, carefully open the wrapping and break off a piece of the chocolate Easter bunny that was perched atop the grass. And even though the one sitting on the bed wasn't eating the yummy chocolate, she could taste it.

The child standing near the basket heard her mother coming and tried to wipe the chocolate off her hand. Her fatal error was wiping it on her Easter dress. Her mother walked in and immediately spotted the streak of chocolate on the dress.

"Did you get into the Easter basket?" she demanded.

The one who was sitting on the bed stepped in to answer. "No, I didn't get into the basket." *She* didn't. She wasn't lying.

Yet, she could see the chocolate on her dress, and she didn't know how it got there.

When Children Are Not Lying

I completely understand that all the evidence indicated I did eat a bite of Easter bunny and smear the chocolate on my dress. If I were the mother in this situation, I could have assumed nothing else except that my child was lying.

Even if I understood I was shifting between these two child selves in my dissociative system, my explanation would have seemed like some fantasy I created to cover what I did. This probably happened more than once; but my mother's angry reaction made it more traumatic than it needed to be.

"Don't lie to me! I can see the chocolate on your dress," she said. "You don't have anything else to wear. You will just have to go to church with chocolate on your dress and embarrass yourself. Don't lie. Say you ate the chocolate!"

I can't even explain the confusion I felt during EMDR therapy as I re-experienced my emotions and feelings. The brown chocolate stain on my yellow dress proclaimed my guilt. But I didn't know how it happened. I truly believed I didn't do it.

"Answer me!" My mother's anger was growing as quickly as my confusion.

"No, I didn't eat it!"

Lying might have been a better choice. I felt myself being shaken. Then I watched as my mother took the basket and threw it into the trash can.

Going to Church with the Stain of Sin

My feet didn't feel connected to the ground as I walked to the car. I crawled in the door red-faced from crying and tried to hide the stain on my dress. It was important not to cry.

Once I reached my Sunday school class, I felt better.

But the teacher noticed. "Are you OK, Jeannie? Did something happen this morning?"

Everything in me wanted to tell someone about the shaking, but this was not a good idea. I decided to only say, "I got chocolate on my Easter dress."

"Oh, that's OK. I bet it was yummy. Your mother can get the stain out. Come sit down and we will get started."

I sat down, but there was nothing in the room except the stain on my dress. I felt like everyone was looking at it. I listened as the teacher talked about how Jesus died for our sins and then rose on Easter. I was glad he didn't stay dead because of my sin.

I wanted church to be over, but we were headed to the sanctuary. I sat beside my mother as the song told me my sin nailed Jesus to the cross. Jesus got nailed to the cross because I got into the Easter basket, got chocolate on my dress, and my mother believed I lied about it. The chocolate stain was my sin. I felt the dark cloud over me. I hated the dark cloud. It never went away.

THE TRUTH ABOUT LYING

Children who experience early trauma have little foundation upon which to build a concept of truth and reality. I remembered being a great "liar" as a child. As an adult, I purposefully set the lying habit aside to live a moral adult life. It wasn't an easy choice since lying was a great survival skill and I was quite ingenious in disguising my lies. Until I went to therapy and fully understood my story, I didn't realize I had developed this skill because of all the troubles I faced as a child.

While working on this book, I was asked about the lying so prevalent in children diagnosed with Reactive Attachment Disorder (RAD). The question (plea) was for help in understanding the underlying reasons behind the lying and how to tell the difference between intentional lying and dissociative lying (in which the child truly doesn't remember). It is possible for both to appear to be "crazy lying." This seemed to be the case when I told my mother I hadn't eaten the chocolate, while the stain on my dress said otherwise.

My lie was a dissociative episode, but I might have also told this blatant "lie" for other reasons—such as avoiding punishment, inability to distinguish fantasy from reality, trying to control the situation, seeking attention, a PTSD reenactment (saying something is happening that is clearly not happening), or as a survival defense mechanism.

As I understood more about myself and my story, I realized my young self was reaping the results of trauma. During the years when I should have been developing the ability to distinguish fantasy from reality, truth from lies, and safe places from dangerous places, there were no clear delineations. What came out of my mouth was based on whatever confused feeling, and whatever consciously or subconsciously perceived need, was present in the situation. I wasn't learning to think critically about my actions; I was surviving out of the "non-thinking" part of my brain. If it helped me survive, then it was truth—my truth. Lying often kept me safe from my mother's anger.

Sometimes my truth meant making up my own stories about what happened to me, what I wanted my life to be like, or some way I could feel safer. I didn't cognitively "know" I was doing this. It was my subconscious effort to survive. My entire pre-therapy autobiography was a version of truth I created because the real story was far too painful to consciously acknowledge.

The word "lie" is defined as an intentional false statement. Maybe we would be better served by acknowledging that most of what we perceive as lying in traumatized children does not fit this definition. In an attempt to remain sane while loving and helping these children, along with a desire to raise moral human beings, our definition may be getting in the way because it assumes intent.

If I am facing a menacing bear in the woods and my only defenses are the words coming out of my mouth, you better believe I don't care if the words are true or not. If I can tell the bear I am a porcupine and it will go badly for him if he attacks me, so be it. I can even become a porcupine if need be! Therefore, the problem is not the "lie" but the trigger (bear) who sent me into survival mode. The problem is, those triggers make no sense unless the story is known.

My truth was whatever it needed to be in the moment the bear saw me. When what I was doing was identified as lying, I learned to become more skillful in my lies. Maybe a porcupine was too outlandish to be believed. My need to feel safe never changed, but my strategies became more sophisticated. By the time I was a young adult, I could convince anyone of my truth—even myself.

It is another cautionary tale. If we place the emphasis on the "lie" and define it as intentional, it will eventually embed itself as a skill set. As an adult, this skill set was still available to me. I chose not to use it—most of the time—but kept it as a super power. Now I understand this super power was the result of survival needs and my subconscious ability to believe exactly what I needed to be true.

Returning to the plea for help: "How do we distinguish between dissociative and intentional lying?" My answer is, "We can't." What traumatized children are saying is often their truth in the moment. We may never know why this alternate view of reality is necessary, but we should consider that it may be an indication of not feeling safe. The child is staring down his or her own personal bear.

This doesn't mean we always accept whatever children say as truth or consider lying as acceptable. There are times I lied and knew I was lying. If I had believed it would be safe to tell the truth, however, lying wouldn't have been my first choice. Other times, the coping strategy of "lying" was subconsciously employed because it worked well in the past and was the only option available. Lying was often a safer option than truth.

There are no simple solutions. In my thinking, the worst option is to call it sin—or to call the child a liar. Sin is most often described as a conscious and rebellious choice. Nowhere in any memories of my childhood could I find a child that the word *rebellious* described. It is far more important to help children feel safe enough to tell the truth and convince them that lying only complicates things (and be sure this pans out as true). This is a long journey for children who have experienced relational trauma and found lying to be an effective defense.

As I processed the memory, Dr. Sue encouraged me to go back to the child and ask what I needed when I stood in the room with chocolate on my dress. My mother's choice to ask, "Did you get into the basket?" turned her into a bear (one I met often).

The chocolate was on my dress. I knew this. How would this have ended differently if my mother merely stated the obvious and let me think about it while she stayed present, but not in my face. This of course would have required a mutual relationship of trust—one in which I was given time to consider the evidence.

What if I reached the conclusion that I did get into the chocolate but didn't remember doing it? This is classic dissociation; but without understanding this, it would seem like another lie. With our present understanding of dissociation, it could have been a chance to help me understand I was not always fully present. The "lies" I told could have been an opportunity for me to consider this—without being shamed for "lying."

Setting aside our presuppositions about intentional behavior is challenging (especially if we have a religious background that emphasizes an inborn sin nature). It is difficult to remain calm in the face of what appears to be a blatant lie. This is especially true when parenting adopted/foster children with severe trauma backgrounds (see Addendum IV).

For children with disrupted attachment and trauma experiences, lying is a given—just as it was for me. Even in therapy, I told lies, but was given the opportunity to process why my "I saw a bear" brain found them necessary. My needs were deep. My bears were so very frightening.

My adult lies during therapy were usually carefully crafted and hard to detect, but they were probably recognized. They always involved avoidance of shame. With the provision of a safe space in which to recognize my own lies, I began to choose healthier strategies when I felt threatened. Learning to climb through a "shame attack," and then choose to honestly express my feelings and needs, was a monumental accomplishment.

Back in the Kitchen

Alice was listening. Everyone almost forgot she was there, until she started talking.

"No one was going to believe I went to Wonderland. Did I go? Or was it a dream? Or did I make the story up? Or was my brain trying to find a solution to something? I never really knew, but it was real to me. I do believe I went to Wonderland."

With this, Alice crossed her arms and looked much like Nine when she sulked. For the most part, no one ever believed Nine, either.

The need to be an adult overcame me, and I asked, "But you

do understand that children sometimes make things up and lie, right?"

I felt my mistake instantly; all eyes were upon me.

Five stood up and put her hands on her hips. Soon all my child selves were standing with their hands on their hips.

The Storyteller, who had been feverishly typing, stopped, leaned over, and whispered in my ear, "Could you rephrase that?"

I nodded yes and looked around the circle. They were defending themselves; this was a positive sign. As I searched for words, feet began to tap. I needed to think quickly.

"Wait! You know I believe you! But we must consider how confusing it was for the adults. Yes, they misunderstood us often. But we didn't even understand ourselves. Most of all, we just needed to know we were loved no matter what. Would that have helped?"

This started a round of storytelling about times when each of them was misunderstood. They grew up in a world that had no comprehension of the effects of trauma. Children, no matter what happened to them, were expected to obey, behave, and keep their secrets while always telling the truth. Do you see a problem there? This was no small task for any child (or adult).

Eventually, they all agreed. The adults were justifiably confused by our behavior. But deep care, conversations, and unconditional love would have helped. I needed to feel safe enough to sort it all out.

The Storyteller closed the laptop and said, "There, that's much better. It is time to head to bed. Alice has fallen asleep in her armchair again. The Eights will need to talk about shame tomorrow."

Alice, hearing her name, woke up and dragged her armchair into the next chapter. The rest followed her out the door and then went in search of their beds.

13
THE PERVASIVENESS OF SHAME

The next morning everyone gathered in the kitchen for breakfast. Alice, who had dragged her armchair to this chapter, was still sleeping; but hearing conversations, she sat up and rubbed the sleep from her eyes.

The Eights mentioned it was their day to talk about shame. Then, adult Janyne began laughing and asked, "Do you remember when I told Dr. Sue I really didn't experience very much shame?"

Nine rolled her eyes. "Yes, I do remember! She didn't know who I was yet, so I couldn't say anything, but I was sitting on the couch next to you and I rolled my eyes!"

Everyone laughed. Sometimes, my denial verged on the ridiculous. It was an indicator of how desperate I was to distance myself from the deep well of shame brewing inside of me.

Shame and guilt are often confused. Guilt says, "I feel bad about something I did." Shame says, "I know there is something deeply wrong with who I am." Shame is what we come to believe about ourselves. Thus, my healing involved both releasing the trauma and reframing the incorrect message internalized by that trauma.

These shame messages seemed to come to a focus during my seventh through ninth years. Developmentally, I had reached a stage of making moral choices—and I believed my choices (based on who I was) were the cause of my abuse. All the memories in which shame was most entrenched, revolved around the church basement.

CREATING THE BASEMENT OF SHAME

While it would be the eight-year-old child self who eventually lived in the Basement of Shame, the shame associated with the basement began much earlier.

I was almost seven when asked to carry a box downstairs. It felt good to be big enough to help.

What I didn't know was this task was a guise to lure me to the basement. The children in the church liked to play in the basement, but we weren't to go by ourselves. I didn't understand this also meant to not go with an adult.

I realized my error much too late. I was the One Who Lives and had no fear. I had subconsciously repressed the memory of what this man had done to me before, because I couldn't consciously remember the trauma and live my life. It was buried in the One Who Cried. Dissociative coping mechanisms, which help children live apart from the trauma, also put them at risk.

The day this memory surfaced, I understood the next split was a result of carrying the box to the basement. I put the memory in a box and began filling the Cave of Memories. The part of Seven who lived, began building shelves with her father's hammer.

Once again, a memory filled a gap. Splits were always the result of trauma. The internalized message was that the abuse happened because I chose to break a rule and was looking for attention.

LIVING IN THE BASEMENT OF SHAME

Before this memory of the box surfaced, I stumbled into the Basement of Shame during a therapy session. While processing a memory, I felt myself open the back stairway door to the basement and descend into the darkness. Not being good on stairs even in bright light, my feet searched each wooden step as I crept slowly downward. Finally, sensing the tile beneath my feet, I turned the corner and stepped into a dimly-lit room. Then I saw her.

She was about eight, with a blonde ponytail flipping back and forth as she hopped from one black tile to the next. She didn't see me at first, but as she got closer she paused and stared at me with her large blue eyes.

I asked her, "What are you doing down here in the dark?"

"Oh, this is where I live. The darkness used to scare me, but not anymore. In fact, my favorite thing is when the teenagers make the stairway into a haunted house on Halloween. Everyone else is afraid in the dark, but not me! I like the dark. I can hide in the dark."

And with this surprising proclamation, she hopped to another tile.

This child seemed eight, but I thought we already found my eight-year-old self who was originally known as the small Pilgrim and later as the Problem Solver. She had listened intently to the story of Pilgrim's Progress during campmeeting to try to find a solution for the dark cloud. Thinking the dark cloud was sin, she went to the altar to "leave her burden at the foot of the cross." But when the dark cloud still didn't go away, she brought it to the Basement of Shame. The dark cloud now seemed to hover over this twin. This twin was holding shame in the basement. It was beginning to make sense.

Then I heard a deep voice. "Why are you down here in the dark?"

We both realized we weren't alone. I stepped back more deeply into the shadow and listened as the conversation unfolded.

"I like it dark," she said.

"You know bad things can happen to you in the dark,"

the deep voice responded.

I felt her freeze. Her body began to respond in uncomfortable, but familiar, ways.

"Are you going to hurt me? You are going to hurt me, aren't you?"

"Whoa! No! I was just teasing you, Jeannie. You know me! I would never hurt you. Why would you think I would hurt you? Did someone else hurt you?"

"Yes, I know you! But the thing is, I knew that other man, too. And he did hurt me where I potty. Sometimes it still hurts." Her words tumbled out, first in relief and then in confusion.

From my place in the shadows, I could feel this man's shock and kind concern. I also felt great relief that this memory didn't end like all the others. Everything in me wanted to run and hold little Jeannie, but I seemed frozen in place as the conversation continued.

"Jeannie, have you told your parents? Your parents need to know this." He sounded like he wanted to cry.

"Yes, I told them. They know. They told me not to ever talk about it." She began sobbing. "And now I did talk about it. I am going to be in so much trouble. Please don't tell them! Please!"

For a second I thought I heard the voice of the angel from the campground, but the therapist's couch was beneath me, and the heat of shame was flooding over me. I wished I had taken off my sweater before we started. Perspiration was dripping down my forehead.

"Can you hold her, Janyne?" asked Dr. Sue.

I considered this might be a good plan, but then the memory kept downloading.

My mother is yelling at me for telling. She says I can't

ever do anything right. She says we will have to move now, because I told.

UNDERSTANDING THE SHAME

I opened my eyes and looked at Dr. Sue. "I thought it was my fault. I have always felt the bad things happening to my family were my fault. But it wasn't true: this was not my fault."

Dr. Sue agreed and held me as I sobbed layer after layer of shame from my body.

We visited shame often and usually found my mother there. In this case, the shame was the result of believing my family needed to move because I couldn't keep the family secrets. And this was not the only secret. But the consistent message was that it was always my fault.

As my mind swirled around this new understanding, it was clear these small child selves had held my shame for a lifetime so I could live. This didn't mean my life was unaffected by the shame. But I was grateful for all they had done.

REFRAMING THE BASEMENT OF SHAME

There is a place in my brain where I made a list of all the triggers I found on my journey of healing—a long list that reminds me of those cartoon scrolls that unroll with a flourish across the floor of a room, out the door and down a nearby hill. The scroll increased in length as I continued to process trauma. I am sure I have not yet discovered all the triggers.

After finding the eight-year-old in the Basement of Shame, I began to identify the triggers that often caused her to run back to the basement. Even with the trauma resolved, there were many things—simple daily things—that caused "shame attacks" because of internalized messages—often triggered by making a mistake. I needed to find a way to help her to not relive shame when I made a mistake. I decided to reframe her now familiar dash to the basement.

I saw her running down the stairs. I had made a mistake about the time of an appointment and, even though it caused me to be early and not late, the error was sending her to the basement. I decided to follow her there.

Rounding the corner at the bottom of the stairs, I found her hopping from square to square on the linoleum floor. She ignored me as I stood in the middle of the floor.

"You don't have to come here when we make a mistake," I said.

She stopped and looked at me with her intense blue eyes. Then she started hopping again. The physical repetition helped her anxiety.

"I have another idea," I continued. "Instead of running here to the dark Basement of Shame, how about if we create a new place to go to when you feel like running. We can make that place high above the basement. It can be bright and cheery, with lots of comfy places to curl up and a window to look outside. We will call it the Attic of Hope."

The hopping child stopped. She seemed interested. I took her hand and we went to the stairs. Repetition and patterns comforted her, so we counted the steps as we climbed. There were eighteen. Another stairway appeared at the landing, and we walked up another eighteen steps to the top. There was a turquoise-blue door with an ornate knob. I turned the knob and pushed the door open. Sunlight greeted us through the open door.

The child spotted a big flowery chair and curled up. I explained how everyone makes mistakes. It feels uncomfortable, but it doesn't mean there is something wrong with us because we made a mistake. Everyone makes mistakes. We can choose to come to this place where we can feel comforted about the mistake.

She snuggled deeper into the chair and said, "I like it better here. I like the Attic of Hope."

During the following weeks, I continued to see her running down the stairs when triggered. Each time, I followed her and took her hand to walk up the two flights of stairs to the Attic of Hope. She counted the steps every time.

One day I saw her run to the landing, but instead of running down the stairs, she paused, thought for a minute, and chose to go to up the stairs instead. We had successfully reframed the choices surrounding making a mistake. She understood she could access self compassion instead of self contempt.

RELEASING SHAME FROM THE BODY

It is easy to believe shame is a mental construct and we can simply "think" ourselves out of it. The example of the Attic of Hope would appear to be exactly this. But my reframing was only possible after we resolved the memory that internalized a false message of shame.

Every shame attack grew out of a traumatic incident. Sometimes it was possible for me to ask myself, "When else have I felt this way?" It fascinates me that each "memory feeling" is slightly different from any other. My subconscious was often willing to take me to the first time I felt that way. It always felt like I was a circling hawk looking for the original memory that caused the feelings. Often the present feeling was unrelated, but what was happening in the present was acting as a trigger and bringing that feeling to the present.

Alice jump up from her chair and began talking as quickly as she could. "That is exactly what happened to me when I tipped the jury box over with my skirt and all the jurors fell about! It felt the same as when I dumped the goldfish the week before. But the jurors weren't going to die because I tipped them!"

> *'Oh, I beg your pardon!' she exclaimed in a tone*
> *of great dismay, and began picking them up again as*
> *quickly as she could, for the accident of the goldfish kept*
> *running in her head, and she had a vague sort of idea*
> *that they must be collected at once and put back into the*
> *jury box, or they would die.*
>
> –Alice

"What a perfect example, Alice! Thank you!"

Releasing Shame and Trauma Is Physical

In a sense, walking my child self to the attic was a mental exercise, but it also symbolically required physically releasing the shame. The energy required to walk up the steps was my visual of this. Releasing trauma and shame is always physical. In EMDR shame pours out of the body as heat, like an extreme flush of embarrassment.

I continued to release trauma and shame far beyond therapy. I recognized it and understood the need for release. One method was through a trauma-informed massage therapist. I could feel where I held the trauma energy and concentrated on allowing my body to release it during the massage.

During one massage, the trauma energy was in my hands that had clung to a tree root to save my life. In another, it was in my legs. One day, to my surprise, I felt shame releasing as heat from what felt like every cell in my body as I began to perspire. I was surprised, but not really. I understand how the body holds shame. This is true for me as an adult, and it was true for me as a child. As the trauma and shame continued to work out of my body, massage increasingly became a form of relaxation.

It is a mistake to separate the body from the mind. Doing that is a westernized, modern-day cultural concept that is reaping a whirlwind of stress and trauma-related illnesses. Positive thinking can only go so far if the problem is inside the body. What we "think" may be what we are, but what we hold is what we become. Holding volumes of pent-up trauma and shame in the body will eventually take a toll.

It is a cautionary tale to those who make decisions in education (often politicians with little educational background). When the length of school days increases and recess times shorten, children lose the opportunity to release pent-up energy—and learning suffers. Increasingly, the researchers are telling us the key to learning is physical activity (though this is not a new understanding). While we need to allow all children to release natural energy, releasing trauma energy is critical. When the bear threatens, the body wants to run. When children can't run, they internalize the energy. It releases through behaviors usually classified as "acting out."

I was fortunate to grow up in an era when we had recess morning, noon, and afternoon; and we spent our after-school time running through the neighborhood. I find it fascinating my eight-year-old child self was always hopping from one linoleum block to another in the Basement of Shame. She understood what she needed. My restless anxiety was likely the trauma and shame trapped inside my body.

Looking up from the computer, I realized my child selves had gone outside to play. Even Alice had left her armchair and joined them. They all understood what they needed—something I was prone to forget as an adult. As I stood to go outside, I noticed the White Rabbit come alongside Alice as she walked across the yard.

'It's—it's a very fine day!' said a timid voice at her side. She was walking by the White Rabbit, who was peeping anxiously into her face.
'Very,' said Alice.

–Alice

Yes, I thought. *A very fine day indeed.*

14
HOW SECRETS SiLENCE CHiLDREN

The White Rabbit read,
'For this must ever be
A secret, kept from all the rest,
Between yourself and me.'

–Alice

I returned from walking with Alice and the White Rabbit and stood looking out the window. Nine was everywhere on her bike. A construction company left a pile of dirt in the field next to the house, and she raced to the top of the hill and back down, again and again. Then she stopped and went to play hopscotch with the Eights.

Healing was difficult for Nine. It felt good to watch her play. I was glad she no longer needed to keep secrets—not her own, and not the secrets of all the others.

Along the path to healing, I stumbled over several child selves who made promises and kept secrets—often at the request of my father who was genuinely trying to care for his family in the best way he knew how.

As I mention in *BRAVE*, it was a lot to ask of a small child. But I felt important when he asked me to keep promises and not tell secrets. At the same time, I inwardly believed the need for them was because of who I was or what I did. This was never my father's intent. His attempts to protect me failed in tragic ways, but this doesn't change the intent.

The problem with secrets is they begin to take on a life of their own. It isn't possible to be completely present while holding a secret. It can almost be guaranteed that keeping a secret will eventually require a lie. Maybe it will require an alternate story that one believes so strongly, the lie seems like the truth.

By the time I was nine, I was adept at keeping a secret. This was when my subconscious created the Storyteller. She should have been a writer, but her life required her to use her talents to create cover stories—and along the way, she lost her voice.

THE SILENCING OF JEANNIE

One day while finishing up a therapy session, I was trying to find someone who could drive me home, when I spotted a child self trying to get out of the office. Dr. Sue watched me begin to frantically gather my things to leave. I could see the child running down a long hallway. She was drowning in shame for staying past what should have been the end of the session.

Seeing my attempt to bolt, Dr. Sue took my hands to continue our work. I realized this terrified child self had no voice—all I could do was cry. I felt the hot release of shame flow from my body. This child self could not yet tell her story, but she did release some of the shame.

I left the office in a daze, wondering what had transpired. A child self had surfaced. But I wasn't sure who she was or why she couldn't talk.

During the session, we had been working through the memory of the Eights in the Basement of Shame. While she was hopping from one linoleum square to another, I sensed there was something else—almost like a side note placed in the basement by an older child. With each hop, she would glance over at a closed door. I was familiar with this basement. She was looking toward the kitchen.

The next day, the kitchen door image would not leave me. A childhood song about a kitchen kept drifting through my mind. I spent the day trying to locate my memories of that kitchen.

The children who attended our church with their parents could play in the basement, but the kitchen was off limits. We understood why—because we liked to go in and get snacks. The adults told us it was forbidden, but they kind of winked when they said it, which made it even more exciting to sneak a snack and not get caught.

The next therapy session, back on the couch, I stated, "I need to go back to the basement and go in the kitchen."

"The kitchen?" Dr. Sue's expression encouraged me to continue.

I told her I wasn't sure why I never mentioned the kitchen, but it was there in the Basement of Shame. I told her the little hopping Eight kept looking at it.

We agreed there was something there, but I wasn't sure what it was. I decided I should go back to the basement and process what surfaced there.

There are three of us in the kitchen. The boy, who is my age, is grabbing something off the counter. He is running out the door and up the back stairway. The other girl and I are looking at the choices on the counter. We hear footsteps.

"Oh, no!" I am diving under the curtained sink.

Across the kitchen from my hiding place, I see my friend, just a bit older than I am, crouched behind the counter.

I see a boy walk in. I think he is there for a treat, but he sees her. He is pushing her and grabbing the food from her. She isn't crying for help. I want my mouth to scream.

I want to climb out from my hiding space and run for help. Maybe I can leap upon the scene like a pouncing cat. Someone inside my head is crying, "He is so strong, he is so strong, he is so strong."

He's gone. I hear his footsteps echo. He is running up the back stairway. I am crawling out from my hiding place.

"Jeannie, you can't ever tell anyone what happened. Do you understand? You must promise me you will never tell anyone. It doesn't matter."

I opened my eyes and sobbed, "I felt so guilty for not helping her! I promised not to tell. If I told, everyone would know that I was hiding under the sink and that I didn't run for help. Anyway, I was sure I would be accused of lying. I just needed to box it up and put it in the place where I kept all the other horrible memories I wasn't supposed to talk about. I was learning to be silent, and my mother would have approved."

It took me a while to sort it all out. So much happened in the basement. First Six carried the box down, then Eight revealed her secret, and now this was the twin of Nine, who we hadn't known existed until the day she tried to run and hide. We came to know her as the Storyteller. And this was how she had lost her voice.

During this phase of therapy, I was sorting out guilt and shame. While Eight felt shame for telling her secret to the man in the basement, Nine felt guilty for not trying to help her friend. Someone needed to help me understand I could not have made any other choice.

The internal messages created in the basement wound throughout my life. I wish a therapist had been available to me as a child to help me understand my childhood limitations and avoid embedding internalized messages about who I was from those things I could neither prevent nor control.

The secrets I kept silenced me, and I devoted my creative energies to survival. My writing as a child was seldom imaginative and most school work I saved seems bland and task driven. No one could have imagined the creativity hidden inside with my secrets.

> *There is no greater agony than bearing an untold story inside you.*
> –Maya Angelou

GIVING ALL MY SECRETS AWAY

I was still staring out the window, watching my child selves play, when the kitchen door flew open, and Nine rode in on her bike. I laughed because it was impossible for Nine to enter the house without her bike. She grinned at me and set the bike against the table. She was thirsty.

I poured us each a glass of water and then poured a third as her twin joined us. In the background, I could hear the song that had inspired us to tell our *BRAVE* story. We began to sing our version with great gusto. "We're gonna give all our secrets away!"

I smiled at my two child selves. "We did that, didn't we? Well, not *all* the secrets. We made choices. No one told us to tell or not to tell. But we broke the silence and ended the secrets."

The two nodded in agreement.

Then with hard-earned wisdom, Nine the Warrior said, "Shame held the secrets. When we told our story, we broke the final chains of shame. Whenever children are safe enough to tell their stories, they can break the chains too. We need them to know this, and then the adults need to believe them."

With that pronouncement, Nine got up, retrieved her bike from where she had leaned it against the table, and headed for the door.

"I believe I will go fly over the rainbow on Bluebird again today!" Nine the Warrior said.

I smiled and waved her out the door. The Storyteller and I needed to stay at the table and write the final chapter for Part II.

Alice returned to her armchair, where she could listen as we worked. We heard her humming the tune to the song about giving all our secrets away. The Storyteller and I decided it was great background music for our work. There were things to consider before we asked our ten-year-old selves to join us.

15
BECOMING MY OWN "MOTHER"

Gaining independence required becoming enough for myself. In many ways this involved becoming my own "mother." Dr. Sue's care modeled how to be the mother I needed, but it was hard to give up the unhealthy self-care strategies I developed as a child. The life I lived despite the extensive abuse was proof of the effectiveness of my dissociative coping mechanisms. Yes, the mechanisms were effective, but they required constant effort just to maintain.

Children in many situations find themselves fulfilling the parent role in various ways. Early on, it became my responsibility to not disturb my mother. Since she was incapable of nurture, I learned to care for myself—in many emotionally unhealthy ways—while trying not to disrupt her life.

The Storyteller stopped typing and looked at me. "This was really hard. Do you think Ten is ready for us to tell this story?"

As if hearing their name, the Older Sibling and Comforter appeared in the doorway and said, "We will help you. It was complicated."

DISTINGUISHING THE PARTS OF TEN
When my ten-year-old child selves first surfaced, and I identified them as the Fifth Grader, they were difficult to distinguish because they didn't seem to follow the pattern of one living and one holding the pain. Instead, they both had the

subconscious role of caring for the younger child selves who held the pain and trauma.

Slowly, I began to realize the Older Sibling was much like the caregiver my eldest brother was to me as a young child. He was around ten at the time of my birth, so this made sense. Dissociative parts can be male or female and because of the modeling of my brother, I usually sense the Older Sibling as a boy (and despite his genuine care, he is always slightly irritated when watching over younger children). The other part of Ten, the Comforter, is feminine. She embodies all I longed for in a mother.

By the time I was ten, my inner turmoil required additional subconscious strategies. The Comforter became my self-care strategy. Her ability to soothe me by "floating" helped me to survive life. This also provided a way to care for myself during the most intense parts of therapy.[1] Without the Comforter, I could not have completed the healing at such a rapid pace.

While I normally only mention two parts of Ten, my sense of her (him) seemed much more complicated. The Comforter and the Older Sibling were internal. The one who attended school, went to camp, and lived on the church property was distinct from them.

While visiting a childhood friend, we explored my haunts at this age; but I felt few connections to the locations. It was as if I lived that year as someone not completely connected to my life. When writing *BRAVE*, this was not yet understood, but I did call this part the Friend Maker. She was the cover personality (host) who hid the other two. She was the one who lived.

Much later, another part surfaced as an introjected mother

---

1. I call this strategy "floating;" but it was different from dissociative floating that felt like I was watching from the ceiling. It may be that "floating" was a freeze response flooding my body with endogenous opioids.

who had little confidence in my ability to control my child selves. This part did not surface until we began to work through the memory involving the cliff and started taking therapy out of the office. She was my critical mother who I internalized and took out into the world with me every day. She was part of my strategy (a very unhealthy strategy) for controlling my behavior.

ACKNOWLEDGING TEN

It was difficult to acknowledge all the ways Ten helped me survive while also saying those survival strategies were unhealthy. It was necessary to heal to a point where my child selves realized life shouldn't be so difficult. As my adult selves healed, they began to understand this. During therapy, I often said I fought to live. I thought everyone lived that way.

The roles the parts of ten played (taking care of my younger self, comforting and soothing, finding those who would care for me, and acting as a monitor and filter) were a developmental necessity; but the methods they chose caused me to be completely dependent on others. I was never going to be enough for myself until my child selves believed in my ability to care for them—instead of their caring for me by constantly seeking out those who would help me.

Since I built self care around ten-year-old children, it was necessary to depend on others. It made sense as a ten-year-old child. It was less than effective as an adult. This dependence was well disguised, but it was there, and it became worse during therapy.

I caught myself looking for someone to help me do things that could easily be done myself. Finally, I determined if it wasn't possible to do something on my own, then it wasn't going to happen. I needed to break the pattern of dependency. This meant my life consisted of doing a lot of nothing for months while my child selves adjusted. Breaking this pattern of dependency was an essential step in healing. Enjoying my life "all by myself" was a slow process that resulted in a celebration when I did something independently.

I Didn't "Float!"

The Comforter understood her role was crucial in helping me survive and it was difficult to convince her I was now the healed adult who could be enough for her. In addition, gaining independence from therapy depended on convincing her I could now be a mother to all my child selves.

It was also crucial to find ways to calm myself that did not involve "floating"—the skill on which the Comforter depended. Playing games on my phone helped and, while this was not a healthy life pattern, it was better than "floating." It worked, and I grew stronger.

One day I called for a therapy appointment to talk through a difficult decision I needed to make. As we sat and talked, I noticed that, even though it was an emotional conversation, the Comforter didn't step in to help me "float." Because of this, I could feel the care and concern I was receiving without drowning in a desperate need for it.

I looked at Dr. Sue and said, "I am not 'floating.'"

She looked at me in the way that always meant she wanted me to tell more, so I continued.

"I called you today because I didn't want to stumble, but it wasn't because the Comforter needed you or I needed the Comforter to soothe me."

She smiled as I continued.

"In fact, I don't remember when the last time was when I 'floated.' It just isn't any longer the 'go to' answer when I have uncomfortable feelings."

The Comforter's care enabled me to survive; but if I was

ever going to thrive, I needed to not be dependent on this strategy created by an exceptionally resourceful child. I had believed that, when healing came, I would no longer need the strategy. It seemed possible I had reached the goal.

When Layers Uncover Layers

With Ten healed and the Comforter was no longer stepping in to care for me, there were still child selves who were not convinced I was enough for them. In fact, we didn't even know Five existed. *She* was very dependent on Dr. Sue, probably more so without the Comforter helping her.

It was exhausting but true. Each layer we uncovered led to another layer. This is especially true when healing dissociative disorders. While all healing involves layers, it doesn't always involve child selves at multiple ages with multiple layers. It can be a long and complicated process.

I was feeling confident, and thus was surprised that healing the Comforter sent me into another processing fury. I eventually realized that she had been protecting me from the pivotal memories upon which this book is based. Specifically, this involved Five and the final memories of Three throwing the blocks.

Healing my three-year-old self was crucial. I needed to be able to scream out my anger. This could never happen until I was no longer "floating," because I would "float" before getting there. Five couldn't risk losing her attachment figure because of her anger. My anger was an indication of something being horribly wrong with me.

Looking back at how the layers surfaced, I now understand the order in which they came. At the time, the surfacing seemed random—but it wasn't. The order of healing came from inside me. The memories needed to surface in an order that provided some measure of safety. Even when I was ready for the next layer, the surfacing was often frightening and the urge to bolt was real. But feeling the pain and experiencing the sensations embedded in the memory is the only path to healing.

Healing is a courageous choice. A therapist provides a holding space for the processing. To fear the dysregulation involved in surfacing memories blocks healing. All healing is painful whether it is physical or emotional. This is a difficult truth to accept and walk through. I wanted Dr. Sue to wave a magic wand, but that isn't how healing happens.

I often thought of therapy as a dance in which I slowly became enough for myself. The night Three cried out, and *I was the one she needed*, was the moment when it was certain I had become enough for her. The dance between dependency and independence had finally found resolution.

While lost in thought about the dance, the sound of small footsteps brought me back to the room. Looking up, I noticed my two-year-old self was standing beside me. Leaning over, I kissed her on the forehead and asked, "What is it you are needing right now?"

"Can I have a cookie?" she asked.

The room filled with the smiles of all my child selves. They knew this meant I was enough. My small self came to the kitchen to ask *me* for a cookie. It was time to talk about the importance of asking for a cookie in our journey of healing; but first we all needed cookies and milk and a good night's sleep.

As I poured the milk, Alice came in the doorway dragging her armchair with her. She had been reading a book in the other room, but she was not about to miss out on cookies and milk!

"This is so much better than the tea party," she said, then bit into her first cookie. "Everyone was really quite mad there."

PART III
HOW MY CHILD SELVES HEALED

*[She] began by taking the little golden key, and unlocking
the door that led into the garden. Then she went to work
nibbling at the mushroom (she had kept a piece of it in
her pocket) till she was about a foot high: then she walked
down the little passage: and THEN—she found herself at
last in the beautiful garden, among the bright flower-beds
and the cool fountains.*

–Alice

Alice's garden sounds much like healing. Just as Alice had to set
logic aside while eating the mushroom, I had to do the same
to become smaller (a child self) so I could enter the healing
garden.

One day, while considering this illogical truth, the song
"White Rabbit" (by Grace Wing Slick) began to wander
through my mind just like the pink-eyed rabbit keeps wandering through these chapters:

> *When logic and proportion
> Have fallen sloppy dead.*

Yes, logic and proportion had fallen sloppy dead; but it
didn't matter, because they weren't horribly useful anyway.
"Thinking" about healing is a cognitive pursuit and not very
effective. My research was helpful, but it did not reach down
into the damage incurred by an entire childhood of not processing emotional pain. It is hard for anyone else to imagine

how much processing was required. The most effective healing involved living out the emotional pain in fanciful ways—like a child.

Part II ended with my becoming enough for myself—for all my parts. Dr. Sue's care for the child selves inside me helped me in countless ways, but primarily this helped open a path for me to accept my inner children. The demonstrations of healing that end this book, could not have happened without Dr. Sue's acknowledgement and care for the child selves who sat on the couch inside my adult body.

During therapy, I could see my child selves peeking through the doors and trying to decide whether it was safe to enter. The safe space they found on the therapy couch poured over into my processing between sessions and is evident in the writing within the following chapters about healing.

Part III begins with a story not yet told then concludes with my own personal examples of multiple paths to healing. There are many doors into the garden, but most involve activities we often shy away from as "un-adult." It is hard to help children (or child selves) unless we are willing to put this shame-bound perception aside and become like children.

It is possible for children to heal from the damage incurred by disrupted attachment and trauma, but we must be intentional. When our focus is on behavior and not on healing, we miss the point. When children heal, their behaviors will change.

16
HEALiNG AND COOKiES iN THE KiTCHEN

Alice and I were sitting across the kitchen table from each other—she in her armchair and I in a less comfortable, wooden chair. We were talking about how muddled our thinking became while trying to make sense of things.

She said, "It felt as if I were the Duchess, which made no sense at all."

> *Never imagine yourself not to be otherwise than what it might appear to others that what you were or might have been was not otherwise than what you had been would have appeared to them to be otherwise.*

–Alice

We both laughed at how ridiculous it sounded; but I knew some of the process writing found on my computer was equally nonsensical. (When I processed as the Storyteller, it usually made more sense.) This chapter and the next are examples of healing through real-life storytelling. They stand together as the processing piece that enabled me to *begin* to take over from Dr. Sue the nurturing role of "being my own mother." This chapter is based on the work completed in a series of therapy sessions that enabled me to begin to process attachment-related dependency.[1]

---

1. Healing disrupted/insecure attachment, while included in this book, involved intense therapeutic work beyond the scope of what is covered here and will be addressed further in future books.

WHO NEEDED ATTENTION

As summer approached, I felt confident that my healing would allow me to move forward with my life. So much trauma healing! Nothing in the landscape of my childhood, teen, young adult, or adult years was now causing me to rumble; but my dependence on Dr. Sue was still evident.

It was true. I was still dependent. I tried to act like it wasn't true. I even tried to tell her it wasn't true; but it most certainly was true. I fought the dependency and need for therapy, but finally returned. I needed help—three sessions to be exact.

The memory I then processed with EMDR was of two-year-old Jeannie standing in the kitchen doorway staring at her mother. She was sad. Her daddy had gone to work at the church.

> *I am standing at the kitchen door. The kitchen is bright, but the dining room is dark with large, wallpaper flowers looking down at me. I can feel my carefully starched and ironed dress. I am sucking my two middle fingers. I am watching my mother. I don't know what to do. My daddy left for the church. I begged him to stay, but he left. I cried. I am sad. Maybe Mommy will care.*

It was just a feeling—a desire for comfort. I was little and didn't have words to express this. The feeling within the memory was pure longing.

> *A cookie. Yes, a cookie will help. I am stepping into the bright kitchen. I am brave. Mommy doesn't like for me to be in the kitchen. She is standing at the counter.*
> *"Why are you in here, Jeannie? You know you don't belong in here."*
> *"I want a cookie."*
> *"You don't need a cookie. Go on, you know you don't belong in here."*

But I do need a cookie! I will ask my brother to get me a cookie. He can reach them. There is yelling. He got caught! He is saying the cookie is for me. She is angry! I am afraid. Now she is shaking me! No! Don't shake me!

I exploded out of the memory in deep anguish. At first my crying was fear, but it changed to anger. Then a feeling of determination grew inside of me. I needed to be smarter and more careful when I tried to get what I wanted. This determination was always part of me. It surprised me to feel it at such a young age.

My mother was never going to be able to meet my emotional needs, but she was still necessary. She fed me, she dressed me, she fixed things when they broke or tore. If I wanted toys, she would need to buy them, and she was the one who took me places I couldn't go by myself. At the age of two she became an object to manipulate.

The clarity this memory brought me was astounding, but there seemed to be more....

My daddy is home from church. He is smiling at me. He asks me how my day was.
"I was sad."
He wants to know why, but my mother is there.
"She is sneaky. She tried to get her brother to get a cookie for her," my mother says.
He is telling me I shouldn't do that. I want him to understand, but I can't talk.

I opened my eyes and looked at Dr. Sue. "I think he smirked before saying I shouldn't do that. It wasn't a cookie I wanted, it was attention. This explains why it is so hard for me to express my needs. It terrifies me. Most times, my requests aren't even what I really need."

The turmoil I felt in the doorway was absolutely overwhelming. EMDR allowed me to re-experience the longing that words describe inadequately. The feeling included fear of my mother combined with my dependence on her. It was need, longing, and fear all wrapped together.

It was about a cookie? It was about something so insignificant as a two-year-old asking for a cookie? My life was filled with the ramifications. I could feel myself standing in that kitchen doorway longing for attention my entire lifetime. It was the longing of a small child who was shaken because she wanted attention. It wasn't my fault. My mother didn't meet my unspoken needs. As a result of her punishment, I internalized the message that something was deeply wrong with my natural need for attention.

WATCHING THE MOVIES OF MY LIFE

My entire life began rolling by me like a movie in fast forward. My deepest emotions were at the maturity level of a two-year-old who needed to come in the kitchen, have her mother put a cookie and glass of milk in front of her, and understand why she was sad.

This was tragic.

This movie was about how a small child learned to take care of herself and not trust anyone to help her. There was a deep longing, and there was also a determination to control her world and get her needs met (with an entire list of strategies she developed). Attachment is really a two-sided coin. The need is on one side, but the strategies used to try to control life are on the other.

Coming to this realization that I had spent my life using the strategies developed by a small child began to spin me in circles of shame. I saw how it played out in my relationship with the one person who did listen and care—my therapist. I could see my manipulation, anger, determination, and fear. The shame poured out of me as I sobbed and said, "I am sorry" again, and again.

Finally grounding myself on the therapy couch and regaining some semblance of composure, I moaned, "I have no idea why you were so dedicated to helping me." We both understood the severity of my attachment issues that released in full force during therapy.

By the time I left the office, I felt I was worth the time invested in me. Yes, I was worth it. That was true of the adult me and it was also true of the small child who stood in the doorway. I had spent my life hating her deep longing and the strategies she built. Now I understood that those strategies were the result of my unmet needs in early childhood and that I was the only one who would ever be fully capable of meeting my own needs.

STILL STANDING IN THE DOORWAY

That night, I awoke again and again to find my two-year-old self standing in the kitchen doorway. She was still looking for someone to finally ask her in, place cookies and milk on the table, and sit down and talk with her.

Cookies reminded me of my favorite children's books, *If You Give a Mouse a Cookie*, by Laura Numeroff. I read this book every year to my Children's Literature classes. In my office I even had a stuffed replica of the mouse holding a cookie.

Something about the story deeply fascinates me. A boy gave a mouse a cookie. The mouse then wanted milk, but the milk would spill and he would need a napkin. It went on from there until the circle was complete and the small mouse would ask for another cookie.

That story felt much like my life. I asked for a cookie; but there was no end to what I needed, and the cycle repeated itself again and again. It was a merry-go-round I couldn't get off. I was forever in the doorway asking for a cookie, but what I needed was attention. I used every strategy I could to get what I needed.

The small child in the doorway wasn't looking for my mother. She stopped looking for her as being someone who could meet her needs many long years ago. There was a long line of those she thought would meet her needs. Many took care of her and most were kind—but some were not, and she would beg them not to hurt her.

How could I convince this two-year-old child self in the doorway that I was enough? I sat in therapy but wanted to be in the kitchen. This took so many forms—some blatant, some sneaky, many "needy" and "manipulative"—all laden with layers of shame. Even when I, like the mouse, received a "cookie," it was never enough. Nothing would ever be enough until I could be enough for myself. Looking to others to fill something inside of myself was never going to be the answer. I had to be the one who invited my child self into the kitchen. I decided to use storytelling to accomplish this.

Jeannie Is Invited into the Kitchen

The next morning, I saw small Jeannie standing in the kitchen door.

"Jeannie! How good to see you at last! Would you like a cookie with some milk?"

She was hesitant. She had stood in that doorway for so many years. I felt the turmoil inside of her—the need, the fear, the longing. I sat down at the table and motioned for her to come sit beside me. She moved cautiously to the table.

We sat and looked at each other, both knowing that the cookies were simply a request for attention.

"Jeannie, I'm sorry all those bad things happened to you. You didn't want any of that. You just wanted someone to care. I needed to grow up, grow old, become wise, work through the layers of pain, and now I can help you. I am sorry it took so long."

She nodded as if to say it was OK and picked up the Oreo (our personal favorite) and dipped it in the milk. We grinned at each other because we knew dipping was so unacceptable. She munched on the cookie until it was gone. I picked up mine and took apart the two halves—also unacceptable. She grinned and asked for another cookie—which I gladly produced. This time, her small hands pulled it apart. It broke, and she looked afraid; but then she noticed my second one also broke.

"They taste just the same even if they break," I told her.

She seemed to relax and asked, "Can I tell you why I was sad that day?"

"Yes! I am here to listen to you."

"Our daddy took care of me. He loved me very much. When he wasn't there, Mommy got upset and sometimes she was mean to me. I didn't like when Daddy left."

"I know. I cried when he left me too. He lived a long time and he was so uncomfortable. I was glad he wasn't in pain anymore, but I cried when he left. I understand why you were sad. He loved us very much."

She looked at me with solemn eyes and took a while to speak.

"Why did he love her when she was mean to me?"

I understood her question. I remembered when my mother died and he grieved so deeply. I wanted him to be happy again.

"Maybe bad things happened to her and that is why she acted that way. She really was mean to us, but Daddy saw the good in her."

"Kind of like the cookie still tastes good even when it breaks."

This part of me was a mixture of oddly mature wisdom and childlikeness. Yes, that was who my father was. He always saw the good in others.

Small Jeannie was getting restless. Cookie crumbs around her mouth were the only evidence of the treat. I handed her a napkin and she handed one back to me. She climbed down from her chair and started for the doorway, then stopped and looked at me. She seemed afraid to ask, but finally did. "Will you always be here when I want to talk?"

"Yes, Jeannie. I am the one and only person you can always count on being here when you need me."

Suddenly, all my child selves were standing in the doorway. They had all felt the longing. Each one took turns standing in the therapy doorway. Now healed, they needed to come and sit down at the table and have cookies and milk with me. It appeared that I might be eating a lot of cookies, but some of them might need to wait for another book.

While I set out cookies and milk for all my child selves, I noticed Alice was reading the children's book about the mouse who wanted a cookie.

She said, "Eating cookies and milk makes much more sense than the Mad Hatter's tea party ever did!"

Everyone laughed, remembering how confused she was by her conversation with the Hatter and the dormouse.

'At any rate I'll never go there again!' said Alice ... 'It's the stupidest tea party I ever was at in all my life!'
  —Alice

"Yes," I agreed. "Cookies and milk are a much better choice."

17
HEALING THROUGH LIVE STORYTELLING

Instead of acting out, act in. When you're triggered, locate where you feel uncomfortable in your body. Place your hand there. Bring your breath there. Tell that young fragmented part of you: 'I've got you. I won't leave you. I'll breathe with you until you're at peace.

–Mark Wolynn

The journey to becoming enough for myself required the deepest acceptance of every fragmented part of me. Becoming my own "mother" meant I needed to understand the trauma, unmet needs, and internalized messages of every child self. To do this required an understanding of my story, but also the processes involved in therapeutic parenting of children with trauma and disrupted-attachment backgrounds.

When Parenting Must Look Different

When working with children with severe attachment needs, it is often necessary for the adoptive parent to be protective of his or her role as the primary caregiver. Children who have known nothing except survival, do not respond in ways typical of children raised in nurturing environments. These wounded children are often least likely to trust the very one who has come into their life to be a permanent caregiver.

I realized this common attachment issue was at the core of why my child selves often sought out Dr. Sue and refused to trust me—sometimes verbally telling her I was not trustworthy. This made sense because I ignored my inner child selves for a lifetime. At one point, I nearly threw them over a cliff. They were quick to remind me of this, and they had a valid point.

Yet, if my goal was to become enough for myself, my child selves needed to depend on me and not on our therapist. I worked hard to learn to be the "mother" my child selves needed; but putting it into practice with child selves who did not trust me was challenging.

A LOT OF THOUGHT WENT INTO THIS!

Live storytelling was how I creatively accomplished the goal of becoming my own "mother." I felt my healing had reached a point that would enable me to carry out this processing on my own—but still have access to support if needed. My growing understanding of disrupted attachment convinced me this was the path to independence.

This processing includes two concepts gleaned from my studies of disrupted attachment. First, it was crucial to remove (symbolically and temporarily) the attachment figure (therapist) on whom my child selves were still completely dependent. They might continue to need therapy, but they also needed to consider me as a viable "mother" figure. Second, if this was going to work, it would be necessary to completely devote myself to their care. Only total devotion would convince them I could care for them; and it was important enough to set everything else aside to do so.

This process was a significant turning point in my dependence on therapy. It enabled me to start caring for myself during "rumbles" far more often. It also helped me realize therapy could end and I would not die. There was no adult logic in this overly-dramatic thinking, but my child selves felt it was a real possibility.

The adult me was living in an RV park. Outside, there were diesel trucks, playing children, and lots of dogs. The sun was shining and the world was drying out from the heavy rain the day before. Inside my RV, I spent an entire week in the "kitchen" caring for my small-child selves. The following is an edited and condensed version of my process writing.

⁓

Realizing story time was ready to begin, Alice entered the kitchen dragging her armchair along with her. To my surprise the March Hare was following along behind her. He said, "I vote the young lady tells us a story."

Alice and I looked at each other in confusion, wondering whom he meant. She pointed to me. "I think he means you," she said. "I think it was a compliment."

JEANNIE STANDS IN THE DOORWAY

It was Saturday and two-year-old Jeannie was standing in the doorway. I felt her ask me to email Dr. Sue, but it was the weekend and we would need to wait until the next week to contact her. It was hard to see Jeannie's disappointment, but I knew this was essential for gaining her trust.

Then Jeannie's expression changed. In her eyes was a mix of both fear and determination. I sensed what she was about to do was going to appear to be "manipulation," and I was right, but I also understood she was only trying to have her needs met.

"Don't you want her to know about what happened this morning?" she asked. "Dr. Sue would want to know how we're doing."

I was not yet enough. What did this young Jeannie need?

I could feel her pain deep inside me. I motioned for her to come to me. But she ran to the bedroom, crawled into bed, and pulled the covers over her head. She was crying as I slid in beside her. She fought me at first, but she didn't leave.

Then terror gripped the small child inside me. I felt the longing as she begged for me to call for help. This was the child self who needed help during the first months of therapy, but couldn't ask. After all these months, I knew I could now take care of her. I held her tightly as she sobbed and trembled. The Comforter crawled into the bed on the other side of us, handed Jeannie the small white puppy, and settled in next to us as she pulled the covers over her own head.

Then sensing what Jeannie needed, I began to repeat, "I will not leave you. I will not leave you…"

Slowly the sobbing subsided; but waves of slow tremors began to wash over me. These were the familiar waves of trauma releasing from deep inside me. My body was trying to calm itself. I held her more tightly as the pain came in waves and flooded over me.

☙

As I typed through the pain, the words fell onto the screen in incoherent letters and partial sentences. It was the pain of a small child with no language to describe her turmoil. Setting my laptop aside, I allowed my grief to flow freely. I was convinced, just like Alice once feared, that I might drown in my tears.

> *But she went on all the same, shedding gallons of tears, until there was a large pool all round her, about four inches deep and reaching half down the hall.*
>
> –Alice

Reframing Childhood as the "Mother"

As my grief and tears subsided, I felt my child self curl up closer to me. This was the first time we had managed to release this level of sadness without calling Dr. Sue for help. I was both relieved and exhausted.

I saw the twin Sevens climb onto the bed. The one with the hammer sat beside me and began to remove more boards from the entrance to the Cave of Memories. The sadness no longer oozed from the cave, but in one corner there was a stack of unopened boxes. I shuddered, thinking there might be more trauma in them.

"Shall we leave them there?" I asked the other twin, who was guarding them.

"No, these are the happy memories we saved for Jeannie. She needs them now. She knows what is in these boxes. They are the clues we kept."

The clues … I did keep clues, but not from when I was so little.

The Keeper of the Cave of Memories, amused at my confusion, explained, "What is in these boxes is everything you loved as a small child. You still love those things when you are just being you. The boxes will open themselves when it is time and you can help Jeannie begin to enjoy life again."

Now that small Jeannie had decided I could be trusted to care for her in her deepest pain and fear, we could begin to build a relationship. This involved opening up the boxes in the cave and re-experiencing both the enjoyable and difficult memories symbolically held in the boxes.

The piece that details this shared experience describes what was found in each box and is possibly some of my favorite storytelling. Yet, I don't want the purpose for this chapter lost along the way. Thus, I have placed the entire story in Addendum V: The Story of the Boxes. (It appears I have turned this book into a "Choose Your Own Adventure" format. You can choose to continue on with the chapter or read The Story of the Boxes and then return here. Or, you can listen to me read the story at my website. Your choice!)

AT THE END OF THE DAY

(I pick up the story at day's end, after our adventures with the boxes. Jeannie needed a bath to wash off the sawdust that had delighted both of us.)

I lifted her from the tub, dried her off with the towel and then wrapped her up tightly as I carried her to the bedroom and found pajamas. She followed me, then, to the kitchen and didn't hesitate in the doorway.

"Can I have a cookie?"

I laughed and said, "Jeannie, yes, you can. But you need to eat some dinner first."

She grinned back at me as if to say, "Well, I tried."

"How about tomato soup and crackers?"

We both loved the Campbell Soup Kids on the can label. I pulled off the label and handed it to her, then opened the can, poured out the contents, and added milk.

Sitting side by side we broke up crackers and dropped them into the soup. We blew and slurped until the bowls were empty. We handed each other a napkin and wiped our mouths. Her tummy was full and her eyes were sleepy. I picked her up and carried her to the bedroom, tucked her into bed, and sat beside her until she was asleep.

I felt good about our day. We shared many memories that are still a part of me. My love for the outdoors, dried clay, sand, mountains, Irises, sawdust and buildings under construction, measuring rooms with long strides, rocking chairs, music, shoes, and all the people who cared about us—not to mention the cookies, candy, crackers and tomato soup! So much of who I am was already a part of this small child who lay snoring in an exhausted sleep beside me.

I hoped our day helped Jeannie understand it was possible for me to care for her. She might be standing in the kitchen doorway in the morning; but for a few hours, she had trusted me. It was a start.

I looked up from my computer to see Alice looking at me. She reminded me of how her sister had seen her at the very end of *Alice in Wonderland*. Her "tiny hands were clasped upon her knee, and the bright eager eyes were looking up."

"It is such a lovely story you have told," Alice said. "I think Jeannie does understand you will never leave her."

"Thank you, Alice. Next time, you can tell a story."

"Yes, just as I requested!" the March Hare interjected. "I vote the young lady tells us a story!"

Alice and I both laughed as she began dragging her chair to the next chapter.

18
HEALING THROUGH LITERATURE

As a child, I wove literature into my fantasies in order to
live above the trauma I experienced.

–Janyne (in *BRAVE*)

An interviewer once asked, "How did your childhood experiences affect the decisions you made in your life?" There weren't many ways it didn't affect me. But I decided to focus my answer on the ways literature wove through my traumatic memories and helped me survive and eventually heal. It is hard to tell whether the literature I read as an adult fit a childhood memory, or did I, as a child, use the literature to create a version of the memory that was easier to accept. Either way, literature was ever present in my processing.

Fantasy plays an essential role in the lives of children. In a review of Bruno Bettelheim's book, *The Uses of Enchantment*, vom Orde states, "Bettelheim puts forward the thesis that fairy tales give children the opportunity to understand inner conflicts that they experience in the phases of their spiritual and intellectual development, and to act these out and resolve them in their imagination."[1]

Literature is an important way children process their experiences. Emphasizing the teaching of reading skills (versus allowing children to simply enjoy the literature) may be

---

1. Vom Orde. H., "Children Need Fairy Tales: Bruno Bettelheim's *The Uses of Enchantment*" (Journal article, 2013). Retrieved from http://ucy.ac.cy/nursery/documents/children_need_fairytales.pdf

robbing them of the fantasies that could help them process difficult life situations.

"Yes," said Alice, who had watched me type the previous paragraph. "I loved to read, but my sister's book had no pictures. This one you're writing doesn't either, 'and what is the use of a book without pictures or conversations?' Well, yours does have conversations. So I guess it is OK."

"Thank you for your approval," I responded with a laugh. "I am glad you have arrived because, per the March Hare's request, I am beginning this chapter with your story from the queen's garden in Wonderland."

OFF WITH THEIR HEADS!

> *Five and Seven said nothing, but looked at Two. Two began in a low voice, 'Why the fact is, you see, Miss, this here ought to have been a RED rose-tree, and we put a white one in by mistake; and if the Queen was to find it out, we should all have our heads cut off, you know. So, you see, Miss, we're doing our best, afore she comes, to—'*
> *At this moment Five, who had been anxiously looking across the garden, called out 'The Queen! The Queen!' and the three gardeners instantly threw themselves flat upon their faces. There was a sound of many footsteps, and Alice looked round, eager to see the Queen.*
> –Alice

Alice did not yet have a full appreciation of the Queen of Hearts' capricious nature. But before long she would understand why the gardeners feared her. The queen's shouts of "Off with their heads!" would soon become part of Alice's Wonderland experience.

There were probably many ways the queen reminded my child selves of our mother. She was unpredictable and held a standard no one could meet. I recognized the connections; but what struck me most were the names of the playing-card gardeners. Each one was named according to the number on his face.

I always thought it curious that, when my child selves surfaced, I gave them age-number names. Most dissociative systems have a variety of names for the parts, but mine were immediately called Three, Four, Five, Six, Seven, Eight, Nine, and Ten. When I said their names, they didn't feel like ages; they felt like names that identified personalities.

"Curiouser and curiouser!" cried Alice.

The pack-of-cards gardeners all looked the same from the back—just like my child selves all wore the same yellow dress. Only the age (number) on the face was different.

> *'And who are THESE?' said the Queen, pointing to the three gardeners who were lying round the rose tree; for, you see, as they were lying on their faces, and the pattern on their backs was the same as the rest of the pack, she could not tell whether they were gardeners, or soldiers, or courtiers, or three of her own children.*
>
> —Alice

Until therapy, I hadn't re-read Alice since my childhood. When adult "me" attempted to read it, it made me uncomfortable and was returned to the library unread. The entire chapter from which the following quote was taken is an uncanny description of how it felt to navigate around my mother.

> *Alice began to feel very uneasy: to be sure, she hadn't as yet had any dispute with the Queen, but she knew that it might happen any minute.*
>
> —Alice

In another section of the chapter, the king's imploring of the queen is quite reminiscent of my father:

> *The King laid his hand upon her arm, and timidly said,*

'Consider, my dear, she is only a child!'
—Alice

But in most other ways, the king is completely unlike my father, who would never hide behind Alice or expect anyone to kiss his ring. Yet, as in my family, the queen was very much in charge!

Finally, there is Alice herself. Outspoken, sure of herself, always taking risks, and somehow finding solutions to things that seemed to have no solution at all. This exchange with the Cheshire Cat is a delightful portrayal of how clever (and hyper-vigilant) I was in navigating my life.

'How do you like the Queen?' said the Cat in a low voice.
'Not at all,' said Alice, 'she's so extremely—' Just then she noticed that the Queen was close behind her, listening; so, she went on. '—likely to win, that it's hardly worthwhile finishing the game.'
The Queen smiled and passed on.
—Alice

Without a doubt, this chapter of *Alice in Wonderland* would have resonated deeply with every child self. Even Ten's decision to get a cat so she would have someone to talk to makes sense in this context. I do wonder if I wished my cat could vanish and be invisible right along with me.

'Well! I've often seen a cat without a grin,' thought Alice; 'but a grin without a cat! It's the most curious thing I ever saw in all my life.'
—Alice

The Nice Teacher

When my own children were in elementary school, the

classic children's book, *Miss Nelson is Missing*,[2] became popular. I never once brought it to the classes I taught on children's literature. But my students did. Even looking at the cover was difficult. *Odd. Very odd.*

I feigned delight over the story of how Miss Nelson, a nice teacher with an out-of-control classroom turned herself into a "witch" substitute named Miss Viola Swamp to help her class learn to behave and appreciate their "nice" teacher. Most often, my odd "dislikes" of something were trauma-related. This book came a tad too close to the truth of one of my stories. The following story, excerpted and adapted from an Attachment and Trauma Network (ATN) blog post, explains.[3]

I was complaining about stomach pain every day. The doctor my parents took me to was wise beyond his era. He told them, "She seems to be a bit anxious about school. Maybe it would help to keep her home for a week."

My first-grade report card proves his advice was taken. In the middle of a year of almost perfect attendance, there was an anomaly. It was called trauma.

I used to tell a story about this year, a story I believed to be absolute truth. I said my teacher was mean, that she tied students to their desks, and some wet their pants. I also said she took students back to the coat area, did bad things to them, and made them cry. Finally, I said I refused to go to school and the teacher was removed from the classroom. When I went back, there was a nice teacher.

Then, in therapy I told this story, but while processing the memory with EMDR, it seemed it hadn't happened in the way

---

2. Allard, H., *Miss Nelson is Missing* (New York: Houghton Mifflin, 1997).

3. The original blog: McConnaughey, Janyne, "The Classroom Through the Lens of Trauma" (June 22, 2017), retrieved from https://blog.attachmenttraumanetwork.org/classroom-lens-trauma/

it was remembered. The way I told the memory was my child-hood perception, but my adult mind was not seeing it the same.

> *I am at school. My teacher is very mean. She is making*
> *my friends stand in the corners. I am trying to sit very still*
> *so I won't be noticed. She is yelling at them and hitting*
> *them. I am afraid. My stomach hurts. I need to stay home*
> *because it hurts so much. They can't find anything wrong*
> *with me, but the doctor thinks if I stay home and rest*
> *awhile I will be better. He is smart! I stay in my room.*
> *No one seems to notice me. Then they say there is a new*
> *teacher. I can go back to school now.*

I later found my report card and discovered the same teacher signed it all year long—there was never a new teacher. Yet, I did remember being terrified in the classroom. But why? What happened?

What happened was additional trauma and the resulting hypervigilance. The child who lived that year was terrified of almost everything. She viewed life through a trauma lens.

The true memory was of a teacher who laughingly said, "If you don't stay in your seat, I am going to have to tie you down." Because I was too terrified to leave my desk or talk to the teacher, I had an accident. The teacher, who was actually kind, would take the children to the back of the room to talk to them because she didn't want to embarrass them—but they were upset, and so they cried.

It was a bit disconcerting to know the story I had told my entire life wasn't true. It was how I perceived what was occurring around me. Understanding that how I interpreted the situation was far more important than the truth, was a significant insight.

As a teacher educator, I have spent a good amount of my career in classrooms. I loved school, never felt safer than when in a school, remembered my teacher's names, and felt most of them liked me. But during this particularly turbulent year, I saw everything differently.

Trauma is a lens. Children who have experienced trauma do not view the world the same way as children who have not experienced trauma. It is not clear why the week at home changed my perspective, but the doctor was wise to suggest the plan.

Just like the return of Miss Nelson, when I returned, the teacher and the classroom were back to normal. Trying to explain my perception probably sounded like lying. But for over fifty years, I was absolutely convinced that what I saw through the lens of trauma was true … and for a small, traumatized child, it was.

THE CAT IN THE HAT

The Dr. Seuss story, *The Cat in the Hat*, has been a childhood favorite for many generations. It was odd I never wanted to read it when teaching children's literature courses. There was something about the mother coming home—seeing her pointed shoes outside the doorway. It made me shudder. Leaving the siblings alone at home with danger lurking didn't seem right.

Then, during EMDR, a memory surfaced from when I was nine. While sitting on the couch reading a book, my brother came in and grabbed the book. When I lunged to get the book, the couch tipped backwards. I flew over it and hit my head on the piano bench. At this point the memory went fuzzy.

Through the fog, I felt my brother nudging me to get up. Our mother was parking in the driveway. There was a frantic, confusing scramble to pick things up and right the couch.

Until therapy, I remembered this as a story of my brother and me tipping the couch and having a war with red berries from the holly bush outside. No one else seemed to remember this happening.

I understand the story in the children's book was similar. Did I use the book to create a perfect cover story for what happened? We were left alone, there was chaos, and then a scramble to put everything right before my mother walked in the door. The picture in my head of my mother coming through the door looks exactly like the illustration in the book, of the mother's shoe.

When my mother arrived on the scene there was a lot of blaming and accusing. I was too dazed and confused to defend myself with clarity. My mother thought I was lying, but my father was angry I was hurt. When stressed, I still rub the exact place of impact on my forehead and my hairdressers know to cut bangs short enough to not rub the spot or I will get the scissors out!

The Cat in the Hat was published when I was four, so it makes sense that it probably was a familiar book. I'm uncertain whether I read the book before or after, but I have no uncertainty about connecting the book with that day and its chaos. The chaos in the book always made me uncomfortable.

GOODNIGHT, ROOM

Towards the end of therapy, while mostly feeling independent during the daytime, my child self still struggled in the night. One night I had a dream that looked like an illustration in the book, *Goodnight Moon*, by Margaret Wise Brown. Published in 1947, this book, with its calming rhythms about ordinary things, ushered in a new form of children's literature that built stories around the everyday lives of children. *Goodnight Moon* has become a classic and a bedtime ritual for several generations now.

During my healing process, I became aware that my sleep had seldom been peaceful. It never crossed my mind that everyone didn't wake up with a start on an hourly basis. I could almost set time on my first startle, which was exactly one hour from when I fell asleep.

After the abuse at three, night terrors were common. Then there were incidents that took place later in childhood and caused sleeping to not feel safe. In addition, my dissociative experiences during abuse often ended with a blinding return to a terrifying reality. This seemed very much like coming out of a deep sleep. Waking terrified me. My mind was never at ease. It would take some time for me to get grounded and ready to begin the day. Sometimes I entered the day in warrior mode, but most often I arrived as a frightened child.

This whole sleeping-waking scenario only seemed to get worse as therapy drew to a close. In the daytime I felt confident and whole—a great relief. But night was a different story, as my sleep became increasingly restless. It occurred to me I was an adult in the daytime but a child at night. The hypervigilant part of me was still standing guard.

Then one night, I awoke to see a dreamlike "Dr. Sue" sitting in a rocking chair at the foot of my bed. She looked just like the woman in the book, *Goodnight Moon*. No matter my position in the bed, I always turned to look for her.

This symbolic "Dr. Sue" made sense. She was the first person to ever help my child selves feel safe. I needed to symbolically keep her in my subconscious so I could feel safe in the night. In the daytime, my child selves seemed completely content with me being their caregiver. But at night, when asleep, they didn't feel safe. We are never more vulnerable than when we are asleep. How could my child selves expect me to protect them when I was passed out in the bed?

The next night, I decided to talk to the child selves who were waking up to look for the symbolic "Dr. Sue." After a couple restless hours, sleep overtook me, but sure enough, in an hour, I woke with a start and looked at the foot of my bed.

Questioning the panicky child self inside of me, I said, "You are frightened. Can you tell me what is frightening you?"

This happened several times as various child selves shared an assortment of concerns. None of them were life threatening, but I could sense the fear resulting from a child's psyche attempting to deal with my adult world.

Finally, I called them all together. "So, you understand this isn't something you have to solve, or take care of, or do. Right?"

Heads nodded yes.

"And you know I can take care of this when we get up or when the problem arises, right?"

Heads nodded yes again.

"OK, one last question. Is there anything Dr. Sue could do to take care of this problem?"

Eyes were staring at me.

We discussed this for some time. Dr. Sue didn't live in our RV, she wasn't part of our family, and she couldn't solve the problems keeping us awake. She could care about us, she could smile at us, she could listen to our adventures, but she could not be with us to protect us or solve our problems. This was not something she could ever do.

I could see they were accepting this, so I asked, "Who can do these things for you?"

"Well," one child self said. "Scott can protect us. He won't let anyone into the trailer to hurt us."

I nodded my head to affirm this truth, then continued,

"And the other problems either aren't your problems or they aren't problems anyone can solve, right?"

They seemed to understand this. They were safe. They didn't need to wake up in fear because they couldn't solve problems that weren't theirs to solve. They didn't need a symbolic "Dr. Sue" to stay with them all night long, because she couldn't protect them or help solve the problems, anyway.

We curled up in bed. I said, "Goodnight, room. Goodnight, moon. I am sending my symbolic representation of 'Dr. Sue' to sleep in her own bed where she belongs."

The peaceful sleep of a child, that should have been mine, hopefully would come to me once again.

Goodnight noises everywhere …

❧

Looking up I realized my earlier reading of the book had put Alice to sleep, but as I closed my laptop, she awoke with a start.

"That was certainly a curious dream!" Alice exclaimed.

The March Hare looked at her and sighed. "Alice, you already told that story."

Alice glared at him. She began to drag her chair to the next chapter.

It was odd having Alice and the March Hare wandering through the pages of my writing. But it kind of made sense, considering how the literature of my childhood wandered around in my head for a lifetime.

19
HEALiNG THROUGH PLAY

*It is in playing and only in playing that the individual
child or adult is able to be creative and to use the whole
personality, and it is only in being creative that the
individual discovers the self.*

–D.W. Winnicott in *Playing and Reality*

N ever underestimate the importance of play in healing—for
adults as well as children. Play is a path to understanding
oneself, a window to learning, and an essential element in
healing. Many forms of therapy involve the creative use of art,
music, and play. All these were part of my path to healing.

When trauma occurs, it often robs children of the pure
abandonment found in healthy play. The play of traumatized
children often takes on a repetitive, lackluster character. In my
story, this was especially true since my perpetrator played blocks
with me to gain my trust. He robbed the joy of play from me.
It was crucial for me to allow myself to play again.

Alice, who had dragged her chair into this chapter, looked
at my dog, Weber, curled up beside me.

"Thank you for getting Weber. Playing with him reminds
me of the dog in Wonderland. But I was much too little to play
with that dog!"

*'And yet what a dear little puppy it was!' said Alice....
'I should have liked teaching it tricks very much, if—if I'd
only been the right size to do it!'*
                                                    –Alice

I agreed: Weber was a great addition to our family. His companionship was therapeutic. Because of this, Scott and I named him after Weber St., where Dr. Sue's therapy office was located. He loved to play but was also proving to be a great writer's dog. He was extremely patient with my endless typing.

I watched as Alice stepped outside and picked up a stick. Weber immediately jumped down from his spot next to me and followed her out the door. I wished her luck, since Weber would only chase the stick once and then sit down to chew on it and run away with it if anyone tried to take it from him. He had his own ideas about playing.

JEANNIE COULDN'T PLAY

My recognition of my inability to fully play coincided with preparations for a Christmas trip to see family. I could not muster any form of anticipation.

This lack of anticipation seemed incomprehensible until I found myself sitting beside my three-year-old self in the corner of her bedroom. She was staring at her toys. We had the same sad stare in our big blue eyes. Though we weren't looking at each other, we understood each other's thoughts.

What happened to us was awful, but what was worse was that our mother didn't seem to love us—not when we were small, and not as an adult. She never played with us—I wasn't sure she knew how.

So, we sat there—small Jeannie looking at her toys and me looking at my trip to Seattle. I sensed she needed someone to help her play. She thought I should be excited about the trip. Neither of us had it in us to help the other. Going on a trip and playing with toys both seemed like so much effort.

"Jeannie, how did you get off this floor and figure out how to play?" I asked. I did have memories of playing after that day.

It was confusing.

She looked at me as if she would speak, but then she began to stare again. The floor felt oddly cold beneath me. I shivered and asked, "Do you need a warm blanket? Let me go get you one."

Returning with the blanket I asked, "Can we wrap up in it together? I need a blanket, too."

She moved closer. Now wrapped together, we felt less like trembling, but we still sat and stared.

JEANNIE NEEDED HER PUPPY AGAIN

"My white puppy is in Seattle."

"Yes, it is. We can get it for you when we go. We will bring it back."

With our belongings in two different states, it was a common problem to not have what I needed in the right place. I was always traveling with random items in my luggage that would be hard to explain—like stuffed puppies.

Jeannie was silent again, and it was some time before she stirred, looked at me, and began to talk.

"I didn't want to eat when we got back from therapy yesterday. I didn't want to get off the floor or play. I really did not want to eat."

"Yes, I made you eat and you threw it up. Scott's tacos were yummy, but you didn't want to eat. Sorry. It was OK to throw it up. But you didn't want to play, either?"

She shook her head and mumbled, "No."

"But you loved to play before that awful day."

"Well, maybe," she said. "Playing was just what I did."

This made sense. Children don't think about playing. They just play. As an adult, I taught about play, conducted seminars on play, informed teachers and parents about the importance of play—but always with the idea of just *letting* children play. One thing an adult can't force a child to do is play. To a child it is like breathing. It is the most natural part of being a child.

No, of course she never would have thought about playing—but I did. I watched others play with children, but couldn't play myself. Setting up play opportunities as a teacher was easy, but it was a cognitive effort. Yet, I did remember playing as a child....

"But Jeannie, you did play. I wrote about all the ways you played as you got older—hopscotch, jump rope, throwing sticks, collecting rocks.... Oh, this is so confusing."

Unexpectedly, the small child next to me was older—the Jeannie who helped me write *BRAVE*.

"You don't understand sometimes, do you?" She looked irritated.

"I guess not. Can you explain?"

"The ones who lived played. This Jeannie never played again, but she understood it was something children do. Her puppy played for her and then the ones who lived played."

The older Jeannie vanished and the smaller child self was looking at me. I continued very slowly. "So, you never played again?" This didn't seem possible.

"Well, my puppy played."

"Wait. Puppy? Like the white puppy?"

"No, he was much bigger. People could only see him as my little white puppy, but he was bigger and he told me what to do."

We continued to sit side by side as I thought. I did know about her imaginary friend, Puppy, but I never considered that Puppy played *for* her.

Then, again speaking very slowly, I asked, "So, you did play, but you didn't play?"

"No, I didn't play. I didn't remember how. Puppy played for me. Then I got too big, and no one would let Puppy come with me anymore. I cried then."

"Ah. *Then* the Ones Who Lived played," I said.

Probably no one ever recognized I didn't play again, because Jeannie figured out ways to look like she was playing. This was how I lived my life—figuring out how to do the things that made me look "normal."

I looked down at Jeannie. "We needed a mother to help us learn to play again, but ours didn't know how to play, either. And now I am a grown-up trying to help you play again, and I don't know how."

Jeannie was watching me think.

I suggested, "Maybe we can find things we both like to do now that we are healing. Maybe we can help each other."

Jeannie nodded yes and proposed a plan. "Maybe we can look for things we like to do in Seattle."

Yes. Having a plan was important to me. With a plan, I could work my way through anything. We both stood up, brushed ourselves off, and folded the blanket. I took her hand, and we went to the kitchen to get some lunch. We were hungry. We needed to eat if we were going to figure out how to play again.

How I Practiced Playing

Before my healing journey began, a friend who was in therapy working through her own difficult childhood, was encouraged to plan play experiences for her inner child. My pre-therapy avoidance of all things "inner child" caused me to be skeptical. Thankfully I set this skepticism aside during my own healing process. It is absolutely necessary to go back and heal the developmental gaps caused by trauma. This is true for both adults and children. Play is a path to healing.

I was fortunate to have a young granddaughter who was super excited her grandmother wanted to play with her. We played with playdough and Barbie dolls, took picture walks, colored, and created props for stories. My Facebook friends enjoyed our adventures together, never realizing that I was in the process of learning to play again.

Sometime later, Scott and I decided to visit the Colorado History Museum. My three-year-old self was excited to find the children's interactive area! We explored all the artifacts and then spelled our name with ABC blocks. I tried (sometimes unsuccessfully) to keep my conversation with my child self silent; but my willingness to play and talk with her was a crucial part of healing. She needed me to play with her, just as I had needed a mother to play with me.

Working jigsaw puzzles was an ever-present part of my healing. I sensed it was helping my brain rewire itself. One day, while considering how children learn to put puzzles together, I realized they worked the puzzle again and again until mastered. At that point, the pieces would fly into the puzzle frame—as if by magic. I didn't think board puzzles would be very challenging, so I decided to do the same thing with one of my favorite 500-piece puzzles. The first time I worked it, it took two days. The fifth time I put it together, it only took two hours! I tried two more times, but never beat that time. I mastered it. I felt the sense of accomplishment deep inside me.

Continuing to play was a challenge. While one child self healed, I would become obsessed with a particular form of play, only to leave it behind as another child self surfaced. What interested me one week, didn't interest me the next. I was speed walking through childhood, but the process enabled me to grasp the importance of play for the mental health of the young and old alike.

I also learned, as did Alice, that when adults interfere too deeply with the playing, they rob the joy from the players. The freedom to play again as a child without my adult self second guessing my childlike choices was a continual struggle. It is another cautionary tale for those who enter into play experiences with children. The queen was a failure at this.

All the time they were playing, the Queen never left off
quarrelling with the other players and shouting 'Off with
his head!' or 'Off with her head!'

–Alice

My Introduction To Child Therapy

Soon after my own therapy ended, I became reacquainted with a former student whose specialty is child therapy. My growing awareness of the work of child therapists propelled my determination to communicate hope for the healing of children.

My introduction to the world of child therapy occurred when I tagged along to the ATTACH conference with a group of therapists. This introduction only provides a small glimpse of the wide range of therapy modalities used by child therapists. It is a field that I am only beginning to research. While sitting in the sessions listening to professionals describe their work with children who have suffered attachment wounding and trauma, I was sure Wonderland had materialized.

If I, as a child, could have accessed the professional expertise of these therapists, *BRAVE* would be a completely different book. I would not have waited until past the age of sixty to advocate for hurting children! Knowing my dad lived to be 100 gave me some comfort. There was still time!

I was on a mission. I visited my former student's therapy office several times while working on a teacher in-service presentation. Her explanation of how sand play was used during therapy fascinated me. I watched several online videos to learn more about this form of therapy and jumped at the chance to participate in a practice opportunity in which dreams were utilized as the basis for the sand-play therapy. I chose a dream I had before beginning therapy, that perfectly described my dissociative system (but which, oddly, I never mentioned to my therapist during therapy).

The sand play experience enabled me to use symbols to tell my dream and concluded by my reframing the dream to illustrate my healing and integration. Being able to use the symbols and play in the sand tray was a breakthrough moment as I felt myself beginning to embrace play in this new form.

The therapy modalities used by child/play therapists hold immense power because they enable the child to process through the natural avenue of play—and often allow them to be able to experience play again. It is easy to misjudge the depth of work taking place through what only appears to be child's play!

The sand play experience also enabled me to create a path to fully integrating reality and fantasy in my writing—in creative, but less dissociative, ways. This is evident in every chapter of this book. Creativity, at its core, is the intersection between reality and fantasy. To combine the two in play provides a necessary release seldom found in our stressful world.

When Adults Cannot Play

A child who does not play is not a child, but the man who does not play has lost forever the child who lived in him.
—Pablo Neruda

My granddaughter and I were visiting a friend who went to her garage and got a tub of dolls left by her grown daughters. While I watched, the friend sat on the floor and played with my granddaughter. As I observed, it became clear to me that I had never felt comfortable with sitting on the floor and playing with a child. Though I was not able to participate on that day, my friend's modeling did help me learn to play with both Jeannie and my granddaughter.

At the conference I watched a video of an adult who was given the task of playing with his step child. He sat staring at the toys in the packet. Somewhere in his life, he had lost the ability to play. Recognizing this, the therapist intervened by modeling ways to play with the toys. In a short time, he was ready to interact with the child.

Both examples of adults playing with children added to my understanding of the importance of the adult's interactions during play. Because of this, and while learning more about child therapy, I became convinced that the parent or caregiver needs to be present during significant portions of therapy. My interaction with Jeannie at the beginning of this chapter is evidence that I had as much need to learn to play as she had. Play therapy in which the parent/caregiver is present provides this helpful modeling of healthy interactive play for both the child and the adult.

THE INVITATION TO PLAY

I looked up to see Alice in her armchair. It seemed she returned from playing with Weber. Evidently Alice had come back when I had placed the symbolic "Alice" in the sand tray as I was describing my dream. Now I remembered her concern about remaining in Wonderland without her toys.

> *I shall have to go and live in that poky little house, and have next to no toys to play with, and oh! ever so many lessons to learn!*
> —Alice

Alice looked serious. "They don't let children play in school, either, you know."

"Alice, you are right! But when *I* taught kindergarten, they learned by playing. Now there are no blocks or housekeeping centers. And now the curriculum is so full, they are no longer able to read hundreds of books a year. Children need that. We seem to have forgotten what Fred Rogers tried to explain to us. 'Play gives children a chance to practice what they are learning.' We need to return play to the schools, don't we?"

Alice nodded yes, and I saw her look up at a floating smile as the Cheshire Cat asked her,

> *'Do you play croquet with the Queen today?'*
> *'I should like it very much,' said Alice, 'but I haven't been invited yet.'*
> —Alice

"You see," I said to the floating smile. "The children are waiting for the invitation to play. We can invite them! It is how they learn, grow, and heal."

20
HEALING BY REFRAMING

One aspect of therapy that fit well with my storytelling bent was the process of reframing. In my words, reframing was reimagining my own memory in ways that removed internalized messages of powerlessness and despair.

The two pieces in this chapter display how processing helped my child and adult selves to work together to reframe emotionally-laden settings. It is interesting that the settings of both memories were in locations that presented themselves as darkness.

What I accomplished in the following reframing was not merely an act of positive thinking. While valuable, positive thinking is a cognitive exercise and does not reach into the depths of emotional material embedded by trauma. It is easy to mistakenly use positive thinking as a strategy to cover pain and bypass healing. It required extensive processing to remove the power from traumatic memories before I could reframe the darkness.

REDECORATING DEPRESSION

You are so brave and quiet, I forget you are suffering.
–Ernest Hemingway

My deepest adult depression was a grown-up version of my small, four-year-old self wandering around her dark home. Depression felt like her aimless, lethargic wandering and sadness. I felt this wandering several times while processing with

EMDR. Finally I said, "I need to help this child by changing the house so it isn't so dark." I was the adult now. It was in my power to change the house.

I see her. She is wandering in the dark house. There are strips of light coming through the blinds, but everything else is dark. I will open the blinds!

There, the blinds are open but the house still feels dark. I hate that wallpaper. Take it down! It's old and is coming down in big sheets. Paint the walls a pale yellow so they will reflect the sunshine.

I like it! It is bright and sunny! Even the green carpet looks better now. What if I change all the rooms? They are mine now. I can paint everything! My bedroom will be my office with all my childhood whimsy now stored in boxes. My parents' bedroom will be mine, and my grandma's quilt will go on the bed. Then Lee's room can be a guest room. Guest rooms need to be blue.

Then the bathroom with the tub that was so frightening. I will remove that tub and replace it with an old-fashioned, claw-foot tub and a shower! There! Perfect!

My books are on the shelf at the end of the hall where I used to lie on my stomach to look at the pictures. Now I want to curl up in a chair to read. These books need to be in my office.

Carrying the books to my office, I spotted Non Janyne still sitting in the depth of depression in her chair in the living room. Setting the books on the school desk my dad refinished for me, I went and took her by the hand and led her to the front porch. "This is where you need to redecorate," I explained.

As if by magic, the house from my childhood and my favorite adult porch blended and became one house. I moved it to the top of a grassy hill and planted all manner of trees and flowers around it. By the time I returned to the porch, Non Janyne had finished decorating.

A checkered, outdoor rug covered the porch floor. White wicker furniture with plump, flowered cushions filled the center. On the table was a tray with glasses and a pitcher of iced tea. At one end of the porch was a newly-painted porch swing almost big enough to be a bed. Just in case the evening turned cool, there was a soft blanket hanging over the back. On a side table was a stack of the books I planned to read.

The final touches were the blue paint on the ceiling to keep the flies away and a large ceiling fan to keep the heat away. In addition, there were curtains to pull closed to block the sun. The lake down the hill from the house sparkled in the sunlight.

It was perfect. Non Janyne was holding the small child's hand as she gazed around the porch and then I watched as the child pulled her to the screen door to show her inside. These two, who spent so many dark days together, loved the reframed spaces in their memories. They would enjoy sharing their redecorated spaces with each other.

In the upcoming days, this processing continued to reframe mental images. As the months passed, my newly decorated spaces brought me comfort and enabled me to embrace the healing it represented in my mind. It wasn't just a memory of my early childhood home, it was a space in which a part of me still lived—a place that I, as a child, had no power to change.

Reframing Internalized Messages

When Seven surfaced again later in therapy, she held a pervasive feeling of not wanting to live. Because so much healing had occurred, it was incomprehensible why I would still wake with a sense of not wanting to live. It didn't feel the same as Four's depression, and it was so persistent that I was sure there was another hidden, internalized message.

Children internalize messages for many reasons. We all walk around with what we came to believe about ourselves as children. When positive, these messages empower our lives; when negative, they diminish us. Sometimes damaging messages are a result of a child not understanding something; but more often they result from thoughtless, angry, or cruel words spoken by the adults in the child's life.

The reframing that concludes this chapter is a story based on a series of therapy sessions. My subconscious had been trying to work on the problem for a long time, and I was surprised by the clever solution of one of the Sevens.

Of Boxes and Decks

Seven clung tightly to one core memory until the end of therapy. One day during therapy, the two Sevens led me to the back of the cave where the damaging message was carefully hidden. The box was open, and I could hear sobs echoing throughout the cave.

The memory was of the day my mother angrily said she wished I hadn't been born. I am not sure this was truly how she felt, but on a day when my behavior was unusually baffling, she voiced her feelings in an extremely damaging way.

Sadly, the part of Seven who held the pain agreed with her. This internalized message was the uneasy core feeling that caused me not to care if I lived another day. It wasn't a desire to die at seven, there just wasn't a desire to live. I didn't think I mattered.

In a therapy session one day, after processing this tragic and deeply held message, the Girl with the Hammer grabbed my hand and led me between two rocks to an exit where the sunlight almost blinded me. To my surprise, I found myself on a magnificent deck. To help her hurting sister, the Girl with the Hammer had found a path through the back of the cave and built a safe space where she and her sister could come and sit on a canopied swing.

Adjusting to the blinding sunlight, I realized the deck over-looked the city of Albuquerque. Looking out, I saw the city spread out below us exactly as it was the day my family drove to Sandia Crest.

"I built this for my sister," she said, glowing with pride. Her efforts were truly inspiring.

I did feel immediately better on the deck. My tears over what my mother had said, stopped. I opened my eyes, looked at Dr. Sue, and giggled. She smiled back as I explained the deck. Some-times my processing took us to the most unexpected places. My subconscious had already been working to reframe the cave.

I left therapy wondering how it all connected. (During pro-cessing, I had imagined seeing residents of Albuquerque waving copies of *BRAVE* at me.) But I did feel so much better about the cave—now that I knew there was an escape route leading to sunshine.

Wanting To Be a Writer

The next morning, I asked the Storyteller if she could help me better understand the twins on the deck. More than happy to help, she began writing.

The twin sister, who was pale from spending her life in a cave, sat silently in the swing. I walked over and sat down in the middle of the swing with the two Sevens on either side of me. There was a slight breeze, and it felt a bit cool. Finding a Navajo blanket on the back of the swing, I wrapped it around us.

Noticing she was holding a book, I asked, "Have you been

asking me to read *Boxcar Children*?[1] Would you like me to read it aloud to both of you now?"

They nodded yes, and I began to read. They had been trying to get me to read this for weeks. Why hadn't I paid attention to the number of times this book had come to my mind? My subconscious was trying to give me clues!

It took a couple hours to finish the book. While reading, I sensed that my early-childhood thoughts of becoming a writer had begun at the age when a teacher read *Boxcar Children* aloud. To my delight, the book included a story about boxes and a hammer. The two Sevens snuggled closer to me while I read that part.

Once the book ended, the Seven twin self, who up to this point hadn't talked, now sighed. "I thought maybe I could write a book like this one someday."

This made sense. But none of the school papers saved from my childhood ever gave any indication of an interest in writing. Everything was typical school assignments—without much creativity.

"Did you try to write?" I asked.

"I did, but I wasn't any good at it. I couldn't spell words right."

I groaned. Her creativity and vocabulary would have been way beyond what she could have written "correctly." This was why my class lectures always implored future teachers to let children write. They would learn conventions along the way. But in the beginning, the endless correcting would kill the joy of the newly-discovered ability to put thoughts into words.

---

1. Warner, G. C., *The Boxcar Children* (Chicago: Albert Whitman & Company, 1942).

Who Was the Writer?

I looked down at the child sitting next to me and asked, "You know we wrote a book, right?"

"No, I didn't write a book. You and the Storyteller did. I can't write."

This made complete sense; but it was sad she didn't understand the Storyteller was an older version of herself.

She looked across the deck to where the sun was beginning to set. She whispered, "All I ever wanted to do was write. I loved letters and how they went together in words and sentences—it was like magic. But I wasn't good at it, and my mother didn't really want me to be born. I gave up."

I understood. It is unlikely my mother thought those awful words every day, but there was no relationship to counteract the message.

The two Sevens held my hands as we watched the sun set in the distance. I could feel the excitement of the child self on one side of me as the sky exploded in every shade of orange around the edges of the clouds. This part of me did want to live, but she spent her life caring for her twin who didn't. She wasn't sure what it would feel like to wake in the morning and not have her sister regret the sunrise.

Keeping Boxes Closed

The night was warm. Instead of taking the Sevens back into the cave, I helped them lie down on the swing and covered them with the blanket. They slept soundly in the warm summer air. As the sun rose over the deck, the twin who had retrieved her hammer, sat up, rubbed the sleep out of her eyes, and waited for her sister to wake. Her sister woke as if terrified from a dream and sat straight up in the swing with panic on her face. She ran for the stairs leading back to the cave and called for Dr. Sue.

She was going to need more help. I returned to therapy where I watched this child self run frantically from one end of the cave to the other.

"I can't let the boxes open! I can't let anything out of the boxes. I can't let anyone see what is in the boxes. But I can't keep them closed! And I need to keep them closed!"

It was a desperate situation. As soon as she shoved the lid down on one box, another opened across the cave like a pop-up game. This was my constant anxiety and I needed to find a way for her to not need to do this for the rest of my life.

The Girl with the Hammer had deep sadness on her face as she watched her sister. She had been able to live because her twin kept the memories from surfacing and disturbing her life. Now she suggested, "We can throw those awful boxes over the edge of the deck." She was figuring out how to reframe the memory!

We all began to gather the boxes filled with betrayal and pain, then we piled them on the deck, and one by one we threw them over the side.

The Sevens paused and set one box aside. They didn't know what to do with it. I understood. This memory was of a person who hurt me, but he did change and spent his life helping others.

Dr. Sue sensed the problem and indicated we could throw over who he used to be.

Yes, everyone deserved the right to grow and change. We agreed. We threw the box over the side. There was no reason to keep the memory of someone who no longer existed.

We watched each box bounce down the cliff and disappear below. Then, I sat on the swing and held the child who had allowed me to live by keeping the boxes closed. The swing's steady motion calmed us.

I realized I was rocking on the couch while I held my child self in my arms. I always had a tendency to rock in chairs. Now I understood what I was trying to do.

In the Night

I thought the processing was finished; but then the twin with the hammer began talking.

"There is more she needs to tell you. In the nights she would sleep, but she couldn't hold the boxes closed, and they would come open and hurt her night after night."

I felt the small body in my arms begin to sob. She had drifted off to sleep and had begun reliving the pain in a dream just as she had always done, night after night. The terror of the boxes filled me as they bumped into me, and I gasped for air in the darkness.

Dr. Sue was rubbing my hands, and the terror began to fade. I surely didn't have to be afraid of the boxes anymore, but could I be certain?

My child selves seemed to feel the same way and, as one, we got up and walked to the edge of the deck and looked over. I sensed we feared we would see the pain crawling back up the side like spiders, but there were only box fragments that had torn off as the pain bumped its way down the side of the cliff.

Sighing with relief, I grounded myself back on the couch, then later headed home in exhaustion. Weary from the processing, I crawled into bed and listened to the music the Sevens loved, as tears began to flow from somewhere deep inside my body.

The Deck of the Living

The Deck of the Living became my place to reflect on how my life did matter. The world was a better place because I was born. I did have a reason to live. I had become the writer I always dreamed of being. My writing was not only helping others; it provided an outlet for the creativity buried inside of me for a lifetime. In the heat of the day, I returned to the coolness of the cave to search for new memories to include in my books. There were so many books in my future!

After the final chapter, Alice would return her armchair to the Deck of the Living, where it would take up permanent residence. She would be there quite often, all curled up and reading a book. Her next adventure would not require the armchair to accompany her. But she was certain that *Through the Looking Glass* was going to fit perfectly in our next book.

21
HEALING TO FORGIVE

Placing this chapter last in the book symbolically represents the process required to reach forgiveness. Forgiveness is commonly considered a prerequisite for healing; but in healing trauma and attachment wounds, many chapters are necessary before contemplating forgiveness.

I entered therapy believing myself to be a forgiving person. The truth was, everything that had required the deepest levels of forgiveness was repressed. Forgiveness was only an illusion.

The stories in this chapter helped my child selves heal toward the point of forgiveness. This involved not only my abusers,[1] but also my parents, and the church to which most of my abuse was connected in one way or another. The first story draws from an EMDR processing of a memory, the others were part of my processing between sessions.

REMEMBERING THE FATHER WHO LOVED ME

My father was loving and supportive, but he often faced difficult choices that impacted me. It surprised me when I found it necessary to find peace with some of his choices. Relational struggles are part of even the closest of relationships.

In many ways, I lost my close connection with my dad

---

1. No victim (especially if sexually abused as a child) should ever be pressured to forgive his or her abuser.

the year I turned ten and we moved to California. He gave up his church to move where my mother longed to live. The new church was not even close to what he left behind. Then, when the new church wasn't what my mother expected, she hated it immediately.

My dad also faced some physical problems that year and seemed depressed. The promise I made to him during the move (to not talk about the bad things that happened to me) wasn't discussed again. The only way I could keep this promise was to subconsciously repress the memory.

Well into the third year of therapy, my ten-year-old self could no longer hold the promise nor the memory in which it was embedded. I called Dr. Sue from a parking lot and blurted out, "I need to talk!"

WE MADE AN APPOINTMENT

I could sense my father's sadness as I began to process the surfacing memory of the promise. In the middle of my consideration of the difficult choices he made that year, a handyman decided it would be a good time to do some repairs on the Victorian house in which the therapy office was located. First a chisel began to scrape back and forth, and then the worker began hammering. I felt another memory begin to surface.

> *"Hello, Jeannie Ann! What have you been doing?"*
> *It is my dad. I feel about seven. I am wandering around the campground while he is hammering bottle caps to secure the chicken wire to the tar-papered exterior of our cabin.*
> *"I was walking. I saw a deer and a squirrel and I saw Mr. Gunstream, I mean Rev. Gunstream. I walked with him, and he talked to me."*
> *"I bet he did, Jeannie. He really likes you. That sounds*

like a fun day. Would you hand me that box of nails?"

I am holding the box carefully as I hand it up to where he is standing on the ladder.

"Can I hammer a nail in?"

"The hammer is heavy, but you can try."

I climb up next to him and he holds the nail and the bottle cap while I pick up the hammer.

"Here, hold the nail with one hand, but be really careful so you don't hit your fingers!"

He's right, the hammer is heavy! I can't hold the hammer and the nail at the same time. The nail and bottle cap fall to the ground.

"That's OK, here's another. I will hold it, but be very careful!"

I am holding the hammer almost at the top... I swing at the nail—and I hit it!

Back on the couch, Dr. Sue and I stared at each other. We knew the sound of the handyman's hammer had taken me to the memory.

Closing my eyes again, my mind drifted across the years and found the times my dad and I built things together. Our final project was when he was ninety six. We built a ramp so he could navigate his walker in and out of our house.

Tears streamed down my cheeks as I felt the bond created between us while we stood on the ladder. Yes, we kept a promise and the silence hung between us; but we were always kindred spirits.

"I was so busy trying not to be my mother that I never realized how much I was like my dad," I said.

Dr. Sue asked me to close my eyes and think of ways I was like him.

"I love to watch buildings being built. We would watch together. We love to learn. We love to read. We love words—

especially if they rhyme. We love to write. We never think inside the box. We love people. People love us...." The list went on and on.

Deep inside my being I could feel who my dad was.

"No, I never lost him. I *am* my dad. If we made a promise, we were going to our grave with it. He promised to take care of my mother, and he took care of her until the day she died. He kept his promise, but it was hard for me to understand when she was so unkind to me. But we were promise keepers. He didn't intend for me to never tell when someone hurt me. I was having such a hard time telling my truth because it felt like breaking a promise."

When the therapy session ended, I knew I had forgiven my dad for the choices he made in situations that were out of his control. I also loved him even more deeply for who he was in my life. He was back in the heart of my ten-year-old self, right where he belonged. The war between being brave enough to tell the rest of the story and keeping the promise not to tell, was over. She could keep her promise *and* be brave.

And I now understood why one seven-year-old twin always carried a hammer in her hand.

Forgiveness in the Context of Children's Lives

All children live within a context. This context may include family heritage, country of origin, racial identity, and religious affiliation/moral code. Understanding the context is essential for unravelling internalized messages. This section draws from the only context I am fully confident in addressing—my own.

My life revolved around the church and most of my internalized messages were in some way connected with my perception of God's role in my abuse. Because of this, my child selves believed: first, that God created them with some defect (shame); then, that God was responsible for what happened to them; and finally, when they decided it wasn't true that God was responsible, then they were angry at God for giving humans free will and not protecting them.

Separating human elements from God elements required deep processing alongside my healing of trauma during therapy. I was not an adult with a spiritual problem. I was a grown-up version of a child who was horribly betrayed and abused. Most church culture platitudes that seem to comfort those who have not been victims of abuse, are mind bending and soul breaking to those who have survived the sins of others—especially childhood sexual abuse within the church context.

Talking With God About What Wasn't the Plan

Nine struggled with the pain she lived through. One day, she and God sat down to talk. Nine began by asking God a question.

"So, God, when are you in control? That is what people say, you know. They say you are in control."

God looked at the child and gently said, "I understand why you are asking this. Bad things happened to you. Men made choices to hurt you. I give every human free will. Some choose to hurt others. It makes me sad."

"But I wanted you to stop them from hurting me!" Nine was clearly angry. "You are God! Why didn't you stop them? Everyone says you are in control. If you are in control, why don't you stop people from hurting children?"

God was saddened, but not bothered, by her anger. She had lots of reasons to be angry.

"Would you want to live in a world where I controlled everything and humans couldn't make choices? Would it feel like I loved you?"

Nine was thinking. "Well, I wouldn't have been hurt in that kind of world, because you only wanted good in my life, right?

"Yes, you are right, I only wanted good in your life. But would you be happy if you couldn't ever make a choice about anything?"

Nine knew she wouldn't like that kind of world. She said, "My mother tried to control everything I did, and it didn't feel like love."

God looked sad.

Nine continued thinking about what God asked her and was quite sure she wanted to be able to make choices. "No, I wouldn't like that kind of world. But couldn't you stop some choices and not others?"

"If I love, then it means I do not control. I am constantly trying to help people make the right choices, but I am not a controlling God like some think I should be. I lovingly give free will to all. Each person has the power to choose."

Nine was thinking. "God, you are right. Choosing does make life better. But if you don't control everything, then what use are you? People say you have a plan; but, you don't?"

God was undisturbed by what others might think was Nine's impertinence. God loved a good discussion.

"My plan is to love you and bring all the good possible into your life."

Nine thought she had God in a corner. "There, you do control things if you are bringing good into my life!"

This time, God knew the explanation she needed. "That isn't exactly how it works. I need humans to do this work for me. I speak to humans and help them to bring good into your life."

Nine stood up, placed her hands on her hips, and stared at God. "The good for me would have been to be protected. Did you not tell anyone to protect me? To not hurt me?"

God gazed at Nine. This was going to be hard for her. Pulling her beside him, he began to explain. "Yes, Nine, I did talk to people. They didn't listen to me. Your parents tried, but there were others who didn't. I begged the ones who hurt you to not make that choice and cried when they refused to listen to me. Humans needed to listen and make the right choices."

Nine looked thoughtful. "They didn't listen, did they? If they had, they would have heard you and helped me, or not hurt me."

"No, Nine, not everyone listens as well as you do. Sometimes they are living out the things that happened to them, but they still could make better choices."

"You know, God, I understand. When I follow what you are telling me, the most amazing things happen. And sometimes, it is clear people are listening to you because they just appear in my life, or help me, or care about me. This is because of you. Dr. Sue was like that."

God was smiling. "You are right. I knew she could help you heal. And you both worked very hard. You did many difficult things to become enough for yourself."

Nine giggled. "You did have it all planned, didn't you?"

God leaned back and laughed. "Well, Nine, I always have a great plan to bring good into the lives of my children. But it depends on human choices. You chose to listen and go to therapy and do the work of healing. You were very brave. I wanted the goodness of healing in your life."

Nine sat silently for a minute before speaking again. "You know, people have this all confused. They think sometimes you step in and protect someone but then choose not to protect someone else. I didn't understand when someone said they were in danger, but God protected them. If that was true, then it meant you didn't *want* to protect me. That made me sad. I even heard people say you let bad things happen to help me grow strong. I was strong before bad things happened, but I felt broken after they happened. What they said didn't make any sense. I could have died, you know. How is that something that makes me strong?"

God sighed. "No, it doesn't make sense. Maybe your story will help them see how saying these things about me hurts children like you even more. Adults aren't right all the time."

"Well, God, that is really kind of obvious, isn't it?" Nine smiled the impish grin God loved.

They both laughed as they stood up and walked hand in hand into the sunset together. Nine realized she didn't need to forgive God. God loved her and had continually been working to bring good into her life. She was glad God wanted her to make her own choices; she was kind of independent that way.

THE EIGHTS SOLVE THE PROBLEM OF FORGIVENESS

Working through the issues of forgiveness was a long process. With my energy no longer expended on working through shame, the twin who now lived in the Attic of Hope became a problem solver like her twin. This was good, because there were a bunch of problems to solve! I found them huddled together and talking about the problem of forgiveness.

One twin looked up as I entered the room. She asked, "How do you define forgiveness?"

This question did not surprise me; I remembered looking up words in dictionaries since childhood. I was curious, though, and asked, "What do you think it means?"

They whispered to each other a second, and then the Problem Solver answered. "Well, we collected lots of shame in the basement while trying to forgive those who hurt us. We were told Jesus wanted us to forgive. But when we tried, we would just get angry again. We felt ashamed that we couldn't forgive."

This was sad. But I needed them to answer the question, so I asked again, "What do you think forgiveness means?"

The other twin answered, "Oh, yes. To not hold a grudge against someone? To not want bad things to happen to them?"

Her sister added, "To want good things for them instead?"

This was impressive. "Yes, that is usually how people explain it. It was a problem, though, wasn't it?"

In unison, they exclaimed, "Yes!"

They were led to trust, then betrayed in horrible ways. It was so unrealistic for them to be expected to forgive when even adults—with much less abuse—found it difficult.

Looking around, I saw additional child selves joining us. It appeared all of "me" was listening and wanted to be part of this discussion with the problem solvers. They looked at Nine as she began to speak.

"I am the one who stepped in and took most of the pain. I was angry. Forgiveness meant giving up the anger. I wasn't willing to give up anger, because it is what made me fight to live. Anger got us up every day. To me, forgiveness would mean to give up what helped me live."

There was a quiet hush as we pondered this. She was right. She fought to live. But she didn't seem to be saying this in anger now. So I asked:

"Are you still angry?"

The room held its collective breath, waiting for her answer. She was our warrior, but she didn't really seem angry.

"No, I am not angry anymore. I needed to be, until we healed the memories. No, I am not angry. I am still strong and want to live like a warrior, but not because of pain or shame."

The room breathed again. She was healed. She was still our warrior, but in a completely different way. She was brave and strong and she would help us tell our story so it could help others.

"So, does that mean you have forgiven?" I asked.

The two little problem solvers sat up straight, obviously wanting to answer for her. "We know the answer!" they said, beaming. "Forgiveness is what it looks like when someone heals. Now we are healed; we don't want to harm anyone. We don't like what they did to us, and if they are still hurting children they need to go to jail; but we aren't angry. Maybe they are dead; but if not, it is just what should happen—yep, they should go to jail. It is OK for us to think they should go to jail."

She was talking so fast, she needed to stop and take a deep breath before continuing.

"If they have changed and are helping people, we should just leave them alone. It doesn't matter to us anymore. Feeling like this wasn't something we could force ourselves to feel, no matter how hard we tried. Trying just made us feel ashamed, and we sent the shame to the basement. Now we are healed, and it doesn't matter. We think this is forgiveness."

There was a murmuring of consensus around the room and smiles on each face. It was a great speech.

I hugged the twins and said, "Well, forgiveness appears to be settled deep inside you. We may have more thoughts on it later; but for now, forgiveness means we are healed, and what others did to us doesn't control us. We don't have to want bad things to happen to them—unless of course they should go to jail to protect other children—but we are not angry. Thank you, Eights! You are great problem solvers."

Another thought came to me. "Do you think bad things happened to those who hurt us when they were children?"

It was Nine who spoke up this time. "I do think bad things happened to them. It didn't mean they had to hurt others, though. We didn't hurt others because bad things happened to us. Well, I suppose we weren't always nice, but we didn't do awful things. They should have asked for help so they wouldn't hurt us. We need to tell people to get help so they don't hurt children."

My child selves began clapping. This seemed a bit odd. But Nine appeared to like their appreciation of her little speech.

"Nine, it seems you might be almost ready to ride right over the rainbow."

She grinned in agreement but reminded me I hadn't quite concluded the chapter.

Alice was looking down at her chair and wondering how flying over the rainbow in her armchair was going to work.

Seven laughed. "Alice, remember, you can leave your armchair on the Deck of the Living."

Alice looked decidedly relieved.

The Mirror of Reflection

Five still looked sad. I sat down beside her. We were both staring at the picture of our mother my father left when he died. Next to the picture was the large mirror we inherited. We looked at our reflection in the mirror—the small, blonde child and the "mother" who loved her. Our eyes were the same. The set of our chin was the same. Our tears were the same.

My child self spoke first. "I am supposed to forgive my mother, aren't I?"

"No," I answered. "I will never ask you to forgive her. When you no longer hurt, then it will feel like forgiveness. Until then, you just need to keep healing."

"It was the shaking. The bad father hurt me, and I didn't

understand why; but he wasn't the one who was supposed to love me more than anyone in the world. I never understood why she couldn't love me."

I held her as we both cried. My entire life was spent trying to not care about my mother not loving me. Other people loved me; surely that was enough. Dr. Sue cared deeply; surely this was enough. I worked through hundreds of layers. I overcame my fear of the Mother Doll. But I still sat crying with this child as I finished this book. I really did understand it was never my fault. I was pretty convinced it wasn't my mother's fault either. But this child still hadn't healed to the point where forgiveness wasn't an issue.

There is so much pressure to forgive. What was more important? To heal?—Or to say we forgive because it is expected of us, or in hopes that it will somehow magically make things better? Was I still trying to forgive myself for not apologizing? Maybe the issue of forgiveness is partially our determination to forgive others so it doesn't add additional shame for not forgiving. Then it is really us not forgiving ourselves.

I looked up to find Alice still sitting in her armchair.

"That was a complicated paragraph," she said. "It sounded like the muddling things I said in Wonderland. I was just a child, and it was all so confusing. Everyone seemed to be talking in riddles. But I was supposed to know exactly who I was and what I should do."

I sat forward in stunned excitement. What Alice said landed right at the heart of the matter. This was the struggle I had throughout therapy: not clearly knowing who I was.

Without a strong sense of self, it is hard to even consider forgiveness. When I didn't know who I was, it was easy to blame myself for the bad things that happened. Since I didn't have love for myself, it was hard to leave my pain behind. I subconsciously held the abusers' shame as my own and punished myself with it for a lifetime.

Yes, I understood. Through my tears I caught Five's eye in the mirror. "Jeannie, we do know who we are."

"We do?"

"Yes, we do. We are who Dr. Sue saw deep inside of us. We are strong and brave. We are creative storytellers and problem solvers. We are explorers, builders, and memory keepers. We are warriors and holders of emotions. We are comforters and caregivers. We are the healed version of everything we were meant to be, and we want to give hope to the world. Yes, Jeannie. We do know who we are."

"So now it doesn't matter that our mother couldn't help us find out who we were, does it?"

"No, Jeannie, it doesn't matter. I felt you the day you wouldn't apologize for doing something you did not do. I know who you are. You are my internal compass who divides right from wrong. I am so glad you are me."

We smiled at each other in the mirror of reframing. With every part of us healed, we finally knew who we were. We stood up, put our hands on our hips, and looked to our future through what now appeared to be a looking glass.

"Is this forgiveness?" Jeannie asked.

"This is healing," I answered. "And at the end of healing, forgiveness happens. Forgiveness is when what is done to us no longer defines who we are."

Alice smiled at us and motioned to another child standing in the shadows. "Dorothy, they get it. They fell down my rabbit hole and now they are ready to fly over your rainbow."

Five and I looked at each other with surprise and anticipation. We were not aware Dorothy from *The Wizard of Oz* had been watching from the shadows the entire time. What an unexpected turn of events. Our future was before us. We were ready to help the world heal, one child at a time.

And with that, Alice dragged her chair to the Deck of the Living and set out through the looking glass to join me in the next sequel.

22
EPILOGUE: A BRAVE TRIBUTE

This poem, written by my publisher after she read *BRAVE*, embodies my purpose for writing these books—to help the world heal, one child at a time. Often that one is our own inner child.

HEALING THE WOUNDED INNER CHILD

You waited while I caught up with you,
*   child in me;*
Till I could see what you could see
*   and set you free.*
You waited with courage and watched with care
*   all while I groped*
To live my life in need of us
*   but vague of hope.*
Your impish ways allowed me glimpses,
*   a coaster ride;*
I caught a laugh, a cry, a sigh—
*   but you played shy.*
The saddened child would rise and I'd
*   be sick and crying.*
Not to be held nor seen nor heard,
*   must feel like dying.*
The needy child would seek attention
*   and want some more*
Of what was offered to fill the void—

a shifty shore.
The frozen child who couldn't move,
    by terror stricken,
Had breathed the smoke and seen the flames
    that raged and licked.
The visioning child would dream of safe,
    delightful places,
To dance with elves and see the smiles
    in flower faces.
The playful child came out with puppies,
    a few friends and babies
Who didn't stay but opened windows
    on sunnier days.
The believing, trusting child heard the Word
    that rescued her.
She led the way for all the others
    who needed Father/Mother.
I embrace you now; I see and hear
    and treasure you.
Let's hand-in-hand run free as one,
    and live renewed.
"Unite my heart to revere your name," *
    O, Lord, I pray.
And "Lead us on a level path" **
    from day to day.[1]

–Catherine Lawton

*Psalm 86:11
**Psalm 143:10

---

1. This poem first appeared as a blog post (January 23, 2018): http://cladach.com/healing-the-inner-child/

Addendum I: Synopsis of BRAVE

BRAVE: A Personal Story of Healing Childhood Trauma is the story of how I, with the help of a skilled and caring therapist, Dr. Susan Kwiecien (Dr. Sue), unraveled my childhood story of insecure attachment and extensive sexual abuse. As a child, my subconscious used dissociative coping mechanisms to protect me from the pain and traumatic memories.

Central to my story was one tragic week when I, as a three-year-old child, was taken to a home daycare where I was sexually abused. Due to my intense distress, my parents took me to the emergency room where the doctor confirmed my abuse, but believed I was young and would forget. The following days were filled with tumultuous interactions with my mother who could not accept the abuse and could not care for me. My vulnerability caused me to be a target for abuse again and again (in many different contexts) until I was a young adult, and despite my parents' efforts to protect me. The final abuse occurred at age twenty three and resulted in a suicide attempt at the edge of a cliff.

Later in life, as retirement age approached, surfacing memories and inner turmoil motivated me to begin therapy. The use of EMDR (Eye Movement Desensitization and Reprocessing) as part of therapy, enabled me to reprocess the repressed memories buried underneath cover stories of escaping danger. My conscious mind remembered what had taken place right before every abuse (standing at a gate, going into a room with three teenage boys, the father of a baby I was babysitting coming home early, being driven to an isolated river, etc.), but not the actual abuse.

During the first therapy session involving EMDR, while working through an emotional childhood memory, when asked to return to my adult self, I responded, "Which one?" In that moment, my three adult selves, Janyne, Non Janyne, and Jane (the Three Chairs) made a perfect three-point landing in my conscious world. This was my introduction to my subconscious dissociative system.

Dissociative Disorders, among the most difficult mental illnesses to heal, often necessitate at least a decade of therapy. It is a complicated process involving multiple layers of multiple dissociated parts. My retirement, and my dedication to processing, enabled me to heal in much less time. During this process, I came face to face with the lifelong effects of early childhood trauma.

The support of my husband, Scott, who plays an essential role in *BRAVE*, was crucial in my healing. The concluding chapters of *BRAVE* provide an overview of healing and the existential crisis involved in deciding to tell my story to the world: a story hidden deep inside of me for sixty years.

Addendum II: Foreword to *BRAVE*

Janyne McConnaughey may be the most resilient of the resilient clients I saw during many years of therapy. She is also a storyteller. From infancy to young adult years, she had held inside all the intensity of feelings, shame, helplessness, and meaning that were part of each experience of trauma she endured. To cope, she repressed memories detached from feelings, unknowingly created personas to hold the feelings and trauma experiences, and rose above the pain to live the life she was expected to live. This explains the two selves she describes at each age. One held the trauma experience and the other "rose above."

The story she tells is the cognitive retelling of intense therapy—a tortuous journey that uncovered layers of trauma experience held with all the intensity of feelings and the meaning of the experience. The therapy used was EMDR (Eye Movement Desensitization and Reprocessing), a therapy treatment recognized worldwide, that targets unprocessed memories, body sensations, and the meaning of the trauma experience, which are held in the primitive, limbic brain where the fight-or-flight instinct and the feeling centers are located. When trauma has occurred, the instinctual readiness to protect overrides cognition, so anything resembling an emotionally-repressed experience can trigger an intense reaction that can feel overwhelming, confusing and shameful.

Experiencing herself as brave at each of the ages as she processed was a critical piece of her therapy. Janyne was an exceptionally brave child, young adult, and therapy client.

Between therapy sessions, she wrote volumes as she processed what emerged from each intense therapy session and prepared for the next session. She bravely stayed with therapy when she wanted it to be done, and stayed until she was able to connect understanding and compassion with all of herself.

Interestingly, Janyne's Ph.D. is in education with Early Childhood as her focus. Now, with this background, she is ready to use her own experience to help others. This involves understanding the child's experience of connection to self and others. When initial attachment to significant others in a young child's life is missing, and trauma occurs, this connection is absent. Janyne's story shows a path to integration and wholeness.

–Susan M. Kwiecien, Ph.D., LMFT, EMDR II, Retired

Addendum III: ACE Study

The Adverse Childhood Experiences (ACE) Study[1] was instrumental in understanding many of my lifelong effects of early childhood trauma. Excellent resources are available online about this groundbreaking research study conducted by Kaiser and the CDC in the 1990s. The following partial list explains the ways my ACE Score of five out of ten affected my life. The relative stability of my life mitigated many potentially-negative health and well-being outcomes detailed by the ACE Study. The higher the ACE Score, the higher the risk of these outcomes (and many more):

- Depression: Pervasive throughout my lifetime.

- Health-related quality of life: There is a high correlation between trauma and obesity, which was a constant issue for me as an adult.

- Financial stress: Embedded survival strategies and negative internalized messages always show up in financial decisions.

- Multiple sexual partners: Vulnerability caused me to be a target, and then I blamed myself.

- Suicide attempts: I attempted suicide the age of 23.

- Unintended pregnancies: A miscarriage may have occurred. Pregnancy was a real possibility.

- Risk for sexual violence: Multiple incidents.

- Poor academic achievement: I was an overachieving under-achiever![2]

---

1. See "Adverse Childhood Experiences" (ACEs): https://www.cdc.gov/violenceprevention/acestudy/

2. Published article: McConnaughey, J., "The Overachieving Underachiever," *Therapeutic Parenting Journal* (ATN, April 2018).

Addendum IV: Adoption / Foster Care

In writing this book, one of my concerns was correctly portraying the challenges and needs of both children and parents (adoptive and foster) being served by organizations like the Attachment and Trauma Network (ATN). I needed to get it right. A similar challenge faces those interacting with adoptive and foster families (teachers, neighbors, church members, case workers, etc.). We all need to get it right.

If we are going to support both parents and children, everyone involved must understand trauma. Children who survive the unspeakable have a litany of defenses that pit them against the very people who are trying to help them. They are often engaging to those outside the family while wreaking havoc at home. I was a very different child to my mother than I was to those in the church. I accept this. It wasn't my fault, but it was true.

My often-misjudged childhood behaviors made little sense without an understanding of attachment and trauma. Viewing behavior through attachment wounding and trauma requires a different lens. What works for securely attached children who have not experienced abuse, seldom works for traumatized children who suffer from severe attachment wounding, often diagnosed as RAD (Reactive Attachment Disorder).

We desire to support these families, but our lack of understanding often gets in the way. The behaviors we observe seem similar (though extreme) to behavior in neuro-typically developing children. All behavior is needs based, but these children only understand survival. They don't "just want their way," they subconsciously believe their life is at stake. This takes many forms.

During therapy, I came face to face with how I was employing triangulation. When triangulating, children distance themselves from attaching to the primary caregiver by pitting other concerned people against them (see Chapter 17). It is a subconscious defense mechanism. Without an understanding of triangulation, it is easy for those in the helping professions, or concerned neighbors, to think there is abuse or neglect. Often, they scrutinize adoptive/foster parents when those parents are truly doing all they can to meet the needs of the child. Only an understanding of trauma and attachment, along with involvement (vs. cursory observations) can solve this problem.

The plea to adopt, especially in the church, pulls at our heartstrings. The choice to adopt, made with the utmost love and good intentions, can turn out tragically without a complete understanding of the effects of trauma and disrupted attachment. Raising traumatized children may not be at all like the dream. Not that we shouldn't try. But we must help adoptive parents enter with full understanding and hopefully prevent missteps that will only exacerbate the problems.[1]

We must believe these children can heal. The loving and consistent days are important in building trust, but when they explode the deepest pain from their broken beings, it is our acceptance of the anger that will help them learn to trust. It took three years of therapy for me to finally understand this.

Just as Dr. Sue believed I could heal, I have watched these parents steadfastly believe there is hope for the children even in the middle of complete chaos. Every trauma parent I have met tenaciously believes healing is possible.

---

1. The Attachment and Trauma Network does an excellent job of providing resources and support for these parents:
http://www.attachmenttraumanetwork.org/

This is true, even for those who have faced the difficult choice of relinquishment[2] when the anger became so violent or the chaos so great that it put other family members at risk. Relinquishing a child is the most difficult and heartbreaking decision an adoptive parent will ever make. It is not because they haven't tried—often to the detriment of other family members. They have received the brunt of the child's anger and maladaptive coping skills and usually have secondary trauma as the result.

We need to support these parents before and after relinquishment becomes a necessary choice. Judging their parenting skills is not helpful. Our informed support may prevent relinquishment, but once the decision is made, our emotional support is desperately needed. It is possible that another family can build on earlier work and help the child heal. When this is the case, it isn't because the first adoptive parents didn't do all they could. We must understand the damage done to these children will never allow them to follow simple paths to healing.

We can help the world heal one child at a time, but it will take a village of trauma-informed adults committed to more than "lots of love." There is no greater gift we can give to a child than healing, but it will be the hardest thing we ever do.

---

2. O'Toole, C., *Relinquished: When Love Means Letting Go* (Parker, CO: Carrie O'Toole Ministries Pub, 2014).

Addendum V: The Story of the Boxes

The following live storytelling provides the complete picture of the care necessary to become my own "mother," and in doing so, become enough for myself (see Chapter 17). Children not only need us to be present while they delight in the world around them, but also need our emotional support during the most difficult experiences. It is in our presence that they learn how to grow, explore, and become enough for themselves.

THE FIRST BOX

Sitting down next to the boxes, I thought about how Jeannie had only shown me memories inside the sad, dark house. I remembered my mother was afraid of the sun and wouldn't have taken me outside to explore the world. Jeannie would have longed to be outside.

Suddenly a box opened and birds flew out, dogs barked, and the sun rose and shone down on me. I looked up and saw the desert sand stretching out for miles until it reached the distant mountains. All around me Iris plants sprung from the ground in all the colors of the rainbow. The hot breeze blew my hair. Over across the valley, rain began to fall. Thunder sounded in the distance. Below my feet the dried and hardened clay was curling up in cracked rectangular pieces. Bending down, I picked up a chunk and felt its silky-soft surface as it crumbled in my fingers.

I carried the box to the bed where Jeannie was sleeping the exhausted sleep of a child who needed to know she was loved. She started to stir, found her two fingers, and began to suck herself back to sleep. Then her eyes opened and she stared at the box.

"Jeannie, when you awake we will look in the box. There are lots of things you love in this box."

She sat up and motioned for me to open the box. It exploded with birds and sunlight, and she giggled in delight. We were transported to the desert world we both loved, and we walked hand in hand across the dried clay. She stooped down to pick up a piece and watched it crumble between her fingers. Then, more carefully, she picked up several more and stacked them one on top of another, grinning up at me with pride.

Her perfectly-starched dress was slightly rumpled from her nap. Outwardly she looked as if she didn't have a care in the world. Her blonde hair blew in the breeze as her blue eyes looked across the desert. My heart overflowed with love for this small child who would figure out how to live life despite what happened to her.

I picked her up, held her at eye level, kissed her on the forehead, and set her on my hip as we walked toward the flower bed. Yes, we always loved flowers, sand, and the sunshine on our face.

The Second Box

I sat on the porch step and watched Jeannie touch the flowers. A bumblebee buzzed by and she watched it without fear. She was too busy exploring for a bee to bother her.

She returned to the dried clay pieces and worked to make the stack higher. I thought about the other boxes left behind in the Cave of Memories. There was so much in this box, what could possibly be in the others?

It seemed thinking about the boxes made another appear on the step beside me. I couldn't force it open; it seemed it was necessary to stumble onto a memory that caused the box to open. Thinking back to when Jeannie cried because her daddy left for church, I looked across the sandy desert where the frame of a new section of the church building was visible.

Suddenly, the box opened with the sound of a saw cutting wood. Jeannie and I both smelled the rich sawdust. Construction projects had surrounded her from the day she was born. It explained how much I enjoyed building things with my dad. Grabbing the box, and calling to her, I motioned toward her stroller sitting beside the porch. We needed to go watch something be built.

I pushed the one-handled metal stroller while Jeannie held the box. She was getting a bit big for the stroller, but it would serve its purpose today. The box, Jeannie, and I all needed to go to the church. We could hear the hammers from a distance.

"Hold the lid down tight until we get there. OK, Jeannie?"

She held the box with determination and soon we turned a corner and the wooden frame of a building was in front of us. The seven-year-old Girl with the Hammer walked toward us and lifted the lid from the box. This time, a puff of sawdust exploded out of the box and settled on all of us. We breathed the scent we loved and then we sneezed.

Our shared sneeze surprised us and we all began laughing. Seven took the box, and I picked up Jeannie. We wanted to walk through the walls of the newly-framed building. Jeannie jumped out of my arms and began to pick up bent nails and small pieces of wood—her treasures for today.

I watched in surprise as her short little legs began measuring the length of the rooms. The ghost image of my dad was visible walking beside her. She took three steps for each of his. As I grew, with just a tiny little hop, it was possible to match his stride of exactly one yard. Walking beside Jeannie, she smiled at me as we began to "measure" room after room.

Jeannie spotted the new stairs to the basement and turned

to back down them. I remembered how my father helped her learn to go backwards down stairs. This is what he saw in young Jeannie; she was born without much fear.

Following Jeannie down the stairs, I stood in the room that would one day become home to my eight-year-old child self. She had been coming there since she was small. How sad this room would one day be the Basement of Shame.

She spotted another stairway and was off to climb the stairs. I quickly followed her with adult concern about the lack of railings or walls. She ran toward the Sevens who were standing near a pile of sawdust. She jumped into the middle of it and sawdust exploded all over them as they laughed and sneezed.

Sitting on a stack of lumber to watch them play, it was clear she would need a bath when we returned home. All the sawdust would wash away down the drain, and I would wrap her squeaky-clean body in a big towel and hold her tightly until she wiggled away.

The Third Box

The lumber stack underneath me shifted slightly. The Keeper of the Cave of Memories had joined me. There was another box in her hands. She handed it to me and ran back to join her twin and Jeannie in the sawdust pile. All three sneezed again.

While considering the new box, I began to see walls around me instead of framing. Then there was linoleum on the floors and paint on the walls. This was my father's office. The Sunday school classrooms were on one side and the stairway to the basement on the other. At the end of the hall was an exit to a dirt driveway.

No longer seeing Jeannie, I started down the hallway to look for her, but came back for the box. It was still closed.

Jeannie was standing, staring into the nursery. When she was small, she was left in the crib crying while her parents worked in the church. They were close by and believed she would go to sleep, but she crawled out of the crib and into the toy box to play.

When her mother came to check on her, she was not in the crib. Spotting her in the toy box, she began to shake her for not staying where she belonged. Jeannie didn't like going in the nursery after that, but she did love the big rocking chair where other mothers rocked her during church.

Standing beside her, I said, "I understand, Jeannie. You have a bad memory here, but there were good memories too."

I was still holding the box as the lid popped open and the sound of babies laughing and mother's singing exploded out. Jeannie did have good memories in this room!

I walked over to the rocking chair and motioned for her to come sit in my lap. There was sawdust on her dress, but we didn't care. Her two fingers immediately went into her mouth as she snuggled close. I began to rock and sing the hymns the mothers would have sung as they listened to the church service from the nursery.

I felt her go limp in my arms. It was a busy day for her. Standing in the kitchen doorway seemed like such a distant memory now. I wondered if she would wake up crying for Dr. Sue as she had so many nights during my healing process. Would she be frightened to wake in this room she feared?

It was wonderful to hold Jeannie close while rocking her. Exhaustion overcame me, and I drifted off, only to awake and find the Keeper of the Cave of Memories standing in front of me with another box. She was a rather relentless taskmaster.

The Fourth Box

With her finger over her lips, I heard the memory keeper say, "Shhhhhh, she's still asleep."

I nodded and looked at the box.

She whispered, "I thought you might need some time to think about this one."

She set the box next to me and promptly left the room. I felt Jeannie move but then heard her sucking on her fingers, and her breathing became slow and soothing again. We were both sweaty in the warm summer air before the days of air conditioning. Her hair was damp and matted to her forehead, but she slept on, while I stared at the box as if willing it to open.

The box was not cooperating, and my eyes drifted to Jeannie's sturdy white shoes, scuffed from our exploring. Her mother would have to add another layer of chalky white shoe polish. She would be irritated. Then I realized *I* was now her mother, and the scuffed shoes would not be a problem. This child was a born explorer. Scuffed shoes were inevitable.

Unexpectedly, the room became crowded with a dozen or more of my child selves all looking at their shoes. Not wanting to wake Jeannie, I suppressed my laughter at the sight of so many scuffed shoes.

Whispering, I asked, "So, you all got in trouble for scuffing your shoes?"

As one child, the heads nodded yes.

"Well, I am fine with scuffed shoes. You don't need to worry anymore."

And they were gone, leaving me with the box and a sleeping child. Looking down, I realized the box had opened. At the bottom were Jeannie's tiny, linen baby shoes.

Jeannie woke with a start but didn't cry out. We were making progress.

"Look! These were your baby shoes!"

Instantly she jumped off my lap and reached into the box to pick up the small green shoes with leather straps.

She walked over to the toy chest and picked up a doll and

quietly worked to get the much-too-big shoes to stay on the doll's feet. Sitting on the floor next to her, I fastened the straps so the shoes would stay on. She smiled a thank you, then left the room.

Sitting next to the toy box, I took a minute to consider the new memory we created for this nursery. A noise outside startled me out of my musing.

"Oh my! She has gone outside!"

Standing to leave, I tripped over box number five.

The Fifth Box

Gabbing the box, I ran from the nursery, down the hall, around the corner, through the church vestibule and out the front door. Jeannie was squatting next to a Juniper bush. She was looking for lizards.

She looked up at me and explained, "If you grab them by the tail, their tail will come off."

I wanted to scold her for coming outside alone, but her fascination with the lizards was completely understandable. We squatted together and watched the bush intently. The box stayed closed, though—. This wasn't about lizards.

Then I saw him. He was about twelve and was walking down the portico with a group of friends. They caught a lizard and one boy was holding up a tail. The box instantly opened. The box was Lee!

I saw Jeannie's eyes light up. "Let me see the tail!"

Lee tried to act like he was irritated to be bothered by his little sister, but he told the other boy to hand him the tail.

"Can I touch it?" Jeannie asked.

"Sure, go ahead." He grinned but asked, "Jeannie, why are you out here by yourself?"

"I wanted to catch a lizard."

"Well, you will one day. But you need to go back inside."

He took her hand and they walked into the church. Yes, the box was Lee. Sixty years later, he was still watching over me.

Wondering what Jeannie was up to, I stood and turned, only to trip over yet another box. Wishing the memory keeper wouldn't just leave them in places for me to trip over, I remembered there were six boxes in the cave. This was the last one, then.

The Last Box

Picking up the box, I entered through the church doors and found Jeannie sitting on a chair at the back of the sanctuary.

She looked up at me and said, "Mr. Counts will be here soon. He always gives me candy."

Unexpectedly, the box tipped sideways, the lid fell off, and a shower of candy filled the floor around me. Jeannie's eyes grew bigger and bigger as the pieces bounced across the floor. She didn't need to wait for Mr. Counts any longer, because I seemed to be the new provider of candy.

She filled her small pockets with the candy and then unwrapped one piece and put it in her mouth. I saw the image of a gentle man sitting in the chair greeting Jeannie, who was just old enough to receive the candy he always kept in his pocket.

He said, "You have to stay here with me while you eat it, Jeannie. I don't want you to choke."

When I got older, he wouldn't make me stay, and I would run off and join my friends. But this Jeannie needed to stay.

I told her, "Jeannie, you have to stay here and eat the candy. Just one piece for now, and we will find a safe place to keep the rest."

Jeannie went back and sat on the chair to finish her candy while I picked up the rest and put it back in the box. She felt loved in this church building. She knew every corner and person. How sad that only one year later someone would enter those doors and betray her trust.

With the candy back in the box, and the piece in her mouth dissolved, I took Jeannie's hand and we walked out the back door where the stroller was waiting. When we arrived home, we put the remaining candy in a jar and placed it on a shelf in the kitchen.

Sawdust fell to the floor as I pulled Jeannie's dress over her head. She climbed into the tub. I handed her the cup while I washed her hair. She poured water over her knees again and again. It seemed to relax her. She was tired, needed to have dinner and be tucked into bed.

It had been a busy day for both of us.

Acknowledgments

Any decision as courageous as publishing *BRAVE* is life changing. There were so many "firsts" involved in the process and there will never be any other moment as thrilling as holding *BRAVE* in my hands for the very first time. Waiting for the responses and feedback produced unlimited angst....

My acknowledgements go to those who helped me through the "new author angst" and gave me motivation to complete this second book. Thank you for believing in me!

Thank you to every person who messaged, emailed, texted, called, posted a picture of *BRAVE* on Facebook, wrote a review on Amazon, or talked to me as you read or finished the book. You helped me know my courage made a difference. Many commented that they enjoyed "the read." Some felt awkward saying this, but I needed to hear that, beyond merely telling my story, I was a writer.

To my former students, thank you for your support as you read *BRAVE*, wrote to me, and sometimes showed up to visit me. In my darkest hours, I feared I would disappoint you with my story—but instead, you have become my strongest cheering section. I poured my life into you and you have proven that to be a very good choice.

My deepest gratitude goes to Jana White, one of my former students, who stepped in to encourage me at a very crucial time and turned the tide in my efforts to tell my *BRAVE* story. The results of this one single extraordinary act of kindness are now reaching around the world and bringing hope to many. Thank you, Jana.

Thank you to all who provided venues for marketing *BRAVE*. This is an ever-growing list, but the following were the first to step up: The Attachment and Trauma Network (Melissa Sadin, Julie Beem, and Laura Dennis), Pathways to Hope (Kiersten Adkins), Denver First Church of the Nazarene, Bridge Builders (Jerry Storz), as well as podcasts/interviews by Patti Shene and Lisa Michaels.

A special thank you to the staff and "full-timers" at Garden of the Gods RV Resort who celebrated with me. Thank you for the hugs and conversations as you read *BRAVE*!

To my publishers, Catherine and Larry Lawton, thank you for believing in *BRAVE* and using your talents to bring my vison to life.

As always, I thank Dr. Sue (Dr. Susan Kwiecien), who still encourages me, gives suggestions as I write, and celebrates the peace in my life.

Words are not adequate to express my thanks to my immediate and extended family members who have never wavered in their support of my writing and decision to publish. Thank you, Scott, for telling me to, "Just keep writing" day, after day, after day.

And finally, to my very patient writer's dog, Weber. Thanks for keeping me company during endless hours of writing and editing. And thank you to Alice for taking him out to play during Chapter 19. Weber, I promise to walk you more often!

ABOUT THE AUTHOR

Janyne McConnaughey, Ph.D., retired from a forty-year career in education while healing from the attachment wounding and trauma she experienced as a child. During therapy, she wrote her way to healing and now is redeeming her story by helping others to understand the lifelong effects of childhood trauma and insecure attachment.

Along with *Brave: A Personal Story of Healing Childhood Trauma*, and the companion book, *Jeannie's Brave Childhood: Behavior and Healing through the Lens of Attachment and Trauma*, Janyne is working to complete two other books in the *BRAVE* series. She also keeps busy blogging at Janyne.org, and guest blogging and speaking for organizations addressing trauma and attachment.

Janyne enjoys full-time RV living with her husband, Scott, at the edge of Garden of the Gods in Colorado Springs, Colorado, and treasures the time she spends in the Seattle area with her children and grandchildren.

To find Janyne online, visit:

Website: http://Janyne.org
Twitter: @janynetweets
Facebook: http://www.facebook.com/janynemc/

"Thanks to such a tenacious, transparent and tender author, we are all afforded the high hope that healing is possible, no matter the depth of the hidden wounds." –Alice Scott-Ferguson

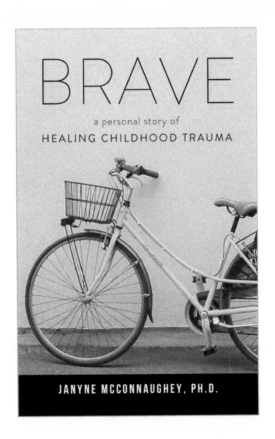

Order BRAVE online and through bookstores everywhere.

CPSIA information can be obtained
at www.ICGtesting.com
Printed in the USA
FSHW010527210119
55092FS